Eight Little words

How God led a Mennonite farm boy to a remote town in Nepal

Otho H. Horst

as told to
Fern Horst & Alyssa Reitz

APPLES *of* GOLD MEDIA
Bealeton, Virginia

Front cover photo, top: Otho as a boy with his parents and several siblings —
(back row) Ethel, Otho's father Otho, Irvin, Otho's mother Anna
(middle row) Martha, Elmer, Melvin
(front row) Mary, Daniel, Otho
Front cover photo, bottom: Otho hiking a trail in Nepal

Eight Little Words: How God Led a Mennonite Farm Boy to a Remote Town in Nepal
Otho Horst, Fern Horst, Alyssa Reitz

Copyright © 2018 by Apples of Gold Media LLC

First edition published 2018

Apples of Gold Media LLC
PO Box 606
Bealeton, Virginia 22712
www.applesofgoldmedia.com

Otho's website: www.othohorst.com

Unless otherwise marked, Scripture quotations have been taken from the King James Version, public domain.

Scripture quotations marked CSB have been taken from the Christian Standard Bible, Copyright © 2017 by Holman Bible Publishers. Used by permission. Christian Standard Bible and CSB are federally registered trademarks of Holman Bible Publishers.

ISBN-13: 978-1717219459
ISBN-10: 1717219454

Lovingly dedicated to the memory
of our beloved wife, mother, and grandmother

Dorothy May Eby Horst

whose devotion first of all to Jesus,
then to her family and all she loved so well,
inspires us to live faithfully in God's plan and purpose
for our own lives until He calls us Home, too.

"Since we also have
such a large cloud of witnesses surrounding us,
let us lay aside every hindrance
and the sin that so easily ensnares us.
Let us run with endurance the race that lies before us,
keeping our eyes on Jesus,
the source and perfecter of our faith."

Hebrews 12:1-2a CSB

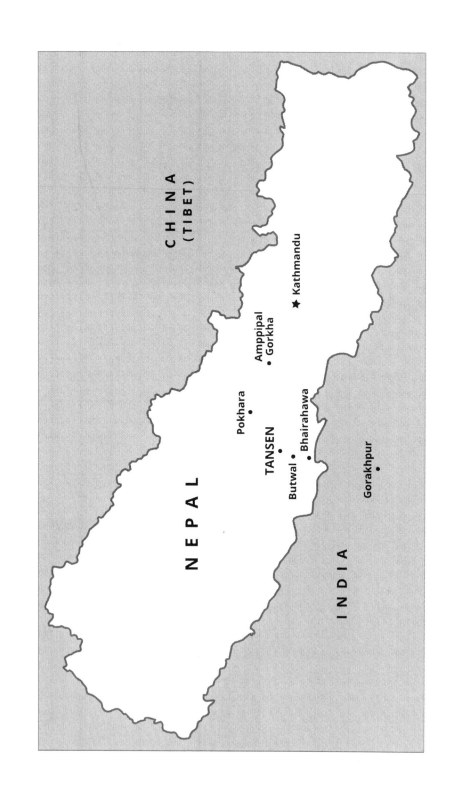

Contents

Acknowledgements

We are deeply grateful to Janice Elder, Janis Holland, Joel Horst, Stephanie Jones, Carna Reitz, and Tim Reitz for their work in editing and proofreading *Eight Little Words* in its various stages. Because of them this volume contains far fewer errors than it would otherwise. Any that remain are our sole responsibility.

—*Fern Horst and Alyssa Reitz*

Preface

Bealeton, Virginia; June 5, 2013

The voice of Otho's youngest granddaughter Valerie broke the silence in the van as she looked up at her grandpa.

"How did you get from being a farmer to a preacher?"

It was Otho's 80th birthday. A group of us were traveling home from a picnic to celebrate this momentous occasion.

"I preached my first sermon the first Sunday in January 1957, in Tansen, Nepal," Otho answered her.

"Did you speak Nepal..." she wasn't sure how to refer to the language of Nepal.

"Nepali?" her sister Alyssa prompted.

"Yes."

"No. No, it was an English service," her grandpa replied.

"How could they understand you?"

"The Nepali people attending that service understood English. It wasn't until later that we held services in Nepali."

"That's when you spoke Nepali?"

"No, I still spoke English and had someone interpret in Nepali."

"Oh. So you had to say something and then wait for them to say it?"

"Right. I would say something in English, then I would wait until they said it in Nepali."

Valerie nodded. She had observed translators in action before.

Otho continued, "Anyway, then I also spoke at different churches when I went down to Sankra, India, to visit the missionary family I met on the ship on the way to Nepal. Let me back up and tell you a little about them. When we left Europe and boarded the ship in Genoa, Italy, there was a problem in the Suez Canal—it was closed due to the war going on between Israel and Egypt. Since we couldn't go through the Suez Canal, we had to go to Rome to fly. Anyway, on that ship, before we got off, we met this family...."

One story flowed into another as Valerie led with questions. Otho transported those of us in the van to Germany, Nepal, Africa, Belize, and many other places as he recounted his experiences. Most of them we had heard him tell before as individual stories. But hearing them chronologically that day within the broader context of his life story sparked our interest in preserving them in written form.

While this volume covers Otho's life to its publication in 2018, we chose to focus on his early years, especially those he spent in Pax (an alternative service to the military for conscientious objectors after WWII). This period seems to hold the most intriguing of his stories, perhaps because they involve a place and time so different from our own. Also, they were the only years he kept detailed diaries.

Those diaries were indispensible in writing this memoir for Otho, as were the letters he wrote to his parents that his mother faithfully kept. We also gleaned stories and information from autobiographical essays Otho had written in the 1990s. Finally, the spontaneous "interviews" we conducted with him while writing were also invaluable.

Otho's life purpose is *"to experience joy and contentment trusting in Jesus and yielding full control to the Holy Spirit, so that with integrity [he] can help others and encourage them spiritually."* That purpose is evident in the unfolding of his life story. May you be inspired to live your own God–given purpose as you read the pages that follow.

—*Fern Horst and Alyssa Reitz, Otho's daughter and granddaughter*

CHAPTER 1

It All Began on a Farm

Clear Spring, Maryland; 1933–1950

*I*n a red brick house on a farm one mile south of Clear Spring, Maryland, a red–haired baby boy was born to Otho and Anna Horst on June 5, 1933. They gave him the name "Otho" after his father and a middle initial "H" to represent his mother's maiden name, "Hoover." He was their sixth child. From 1926 to 1945, his mother gave birth to fourteen children: Irvin, Martha, Elmer, Melvin, Mary,

The Horst family farm located on Route 68 south of Clear Spring, Maryland, just west of Ashton Road.

Otho, Daniel, Ethel, James, Mark, Lois, Luke, Amos, and Samuel. James and Samuel died as infants.

Otho and his siblings grew up on the same farm where their father was born and raised. As it was for many during those post–Depression years, finances were tight for the Horst family. Living on a farm and raising their own food meant they always had plenty to eat even if they didn't have much cash. But it also meant a lot of work to feed so many. His parents worked from dawn to dusk, and so did the children, according to their individual ability. They raised Guernsey dairy cows and owned a milk route. Many mornings Otho and his siblings got up early to milk cows, bottle the milk, and deliver it to homes and businesses before school. After school they would wash the milk bottles to prepare for the next day.

Otho as a baby with his parents and siblings: Mary held by Otho's father Otho, Otho held by his mother Anna, Elmer, Melvin, Irvin, and Martha

In 1939 Otho entered the first grade at Clear Spring Elementary School. He would sometimes arrive late because of his morning chores. When this happened his father would drive his children to school at the end of their milk route. They would jump out of the panel truck they used to deliver milk and hurry into the building to their classrooms.

One morning his teacher said to him, "This is happening more often. Do you think it will get better or worse?"

"Probably worse," Otho admitted truthfully, "because we've picked up more customers."

"I was afraid of that," his teacher sighed. She never brought it up again, knowing this was typical for a farm family making ends meet.

On another occasion Otho learned from a classmate that their teacher had explained that Otho was often late because of all the chores he had to accomplish before coming to school. She reprimanded some students for not getting their homework done when they didn't have nearly as much work to do at home. Otho was grateful to have such understanding teachers.

The State of Maryland required children to attend school until they were fourteen. When Otho reached that age he quit school, just as his older brothers and sisters had done. He thought he knew everything he needed to know to be a farmer, which he intended to be all his life. Besides, he was needed at home on the farm, and both he and his parents thought working at home was a better use of his time. He was glad to be done with school. Later in life he wished he had finished high school. Otho eventually took the GED test and received his high school diploma. He also took several college courses over the years.

Although Otho and his siblings worked hard, they also had a lot of fun growing up together. Years later his wife Dorothy would express gratitude that he survived childhood as she listened to their stories — adventures that were often a mix of work and play and sometimes involved more imagination than common sense.

His father, whom they called "Pop," often said, "If you send one boy to do a job, you get a boy's worth of work done. If you send two, you get half a boy's worth of work done. And if you send three or more, nothing gets done." As the father of eight boys, Pop had many examples to back up his theory.

One day Pop told Otho and his older brothers to take a large rear tractor tire to Clear Spring to get it fixed. They loaded it onto a flatbed wagon and pulled it with another tractor to the garage in Clear Spring. Arriving home, they stopped at the top of the hill at the entry to their lane. Removing the just-fixed tire off the bed of the wagon, they sent it rolling down the lane by itself. It picked up speed, going faster and faster as it passed their house, the car shed, and the chicken house. Now at top speed, it hit the gate at the end of the lane so hard it bounced up in the air and over it, finally stopping and falling over when it hit the silo.

Pop came home some time later and walked into the house. "What happened to the silo gate?" he asked his boys.

Their Grandmother Horst, who lived with them, spoke up before they could answer. Her poor eyesight had mistaken the object flying past the window for something more plausible than a runaway tractor tire. She told Pop, "I saw a deer running down the lane and into the gate."

The boys kept quiet as Pop accepted her answer. A relieved Otho and his brothers fixed the gate and nothing more was said. Years later when they were recounting stories from their childhood, they recalled this incident in Pop's presence. "I never heard that before!" Pop said. By then they were too old to be punished, and they all had a good laugh, including Pop.

Another time Otho and some of his sisters and younger brothers took one of the flat-bed hay wagons up to the end of the lane where they unhooked it from the tractor and tied two ropes to the wagon tongue. One child held one of the ropes and stood on the right front corner of the wagon while another took hold of the other rope and stood on the left front corner. This was their clever plan to steer it down the hill on the road toward Clear Spring.

They were picking up speed and enjoying the ride when they saw a car coming. They decided it would be best to get off the road out of

Otho with six of his seven brothers: (back) Elmer, Melvin; (middle) Otho, Daniel; (front) Luke, Amos, and Mark

its way. There was only one problem — they didn't have brakes. Their only option was to steer the wagon into the bank on the side of the road to force it to stop. It hit the ground with force, running up the bank and dumping its passengers onto the ground. It shook them up, but they were all okay. They trekked back to the farm for the tractor and pulled the wagon home the proper way. It scared them enough they never tried that again.

When Pop went to town, he gave the children chores to do while he was away. But as he disappeared out the lane, they would make a beeline to the pasture field to play ball. They knew their father well enough to know he would get to talking with friends and neighbors and take a while to return home. But on one occasion, they miscalculated how long he would be gone. They heard a car coming up the hill from Clear Spring and looked to see who it was. It was Pop! They took off to the barn as fast as they could and started working. But it was too late. Pop had seen them and gave them all a good spanking.

Pop was a harsh disciplinarian at times. Raising twelve children in post–Depression years had its difficulties, and his temper sometimes got the best of him. But he loved his family and did what he could to raise them to be responsible men and women and to follow Christ. In Otho's last conversation with his father not long before Pop died in an auto accident in 1975, he told Otho how grateful he was that all of his children were serving the Lord. He softened as he grew older and was a loving and teasing Grandpap, leaving his grandchildren with fond memories of fun times spent with him.

Otho's mother was a sweet, gentle, hard-working woman. She softened their childhood with her love and intervened when she thought her husband's discipline was too harsh.

The only time Otho remembers his mother physically disciplining him was once when she asked him to do something, and he ran out the door yelling, "I'm not going to!"

He did do what she'd asked, but when he came back into the house later, his mother said to him, "Otho, come here." She took him over to the stairs and sat down. Turning him over her knee, she spanked him with a paddle. "Don't you ever talk back to me again," she told him, and Otho never did.

She was supportive of her children into adulthood and welcomed their spouses into the family with open arms. She was the epitome of a loving Grandma. Lots of love, laughter, and an abundance of delicious food characterized family gatherings at her house. She was a wonderful hostess, warmly welcoming family, friends, and strangers alike into her home. It was not unusual to find friends of family members at her dinner table.

Otho remembers that she always had plenty of food prepared for visitors who would drop in to visit during his childhood years. He could never understand how she and his sisters could prepare a meal so quickly for so many people. Almost every Sunday, she would invite guests home for dinner after church. Otho and his siblings liked having guests most when it was a family with children their age.

They also enjoyed the many Sundays their Aunt Ruth (their father's sister), Uncle Joe, and cousins Miriam, Paul, Joyce, Merle, Ruth, and Leon came to visit from Lancaster, Pennsylvania. They didn't have a phone in those days, but that didn't keep Otho's mother from being prepared. She would sometimes tell her daughters, "I have a feeling Aunt Ruth will come tomorrow," and they would get busy baking lots of pies and preparing other wonderful food. Sure enough, the next day, Aunt Ruth and her family would drive in the lane.

Otho loved growing up on the farm. One of his earliest memories was when he was five years old. Pop lifted him onto the back of an old gray mare named Daisy and showed him how to drive the horses to harrow the plowed field so they could plant corn. Old Daisy was a gentle, slow, easy–going lead horse, and his father could trust her to let the children ride her.

Otho enjoyed the horses and took every opportunity he could to work them. One day, he was raking hay with a dump rake pulled by two horses. When it was time to unhitch for dinner, Otho was too

Baby Otho and his five older siblings: (back) Melvin, Mary; (middle) Elmer, Irvin, Martha; (front) Otho

small to reach the breast chains, so he walked up the tongue of the rake between the horses to unhook them. Holding onto the hame (part of the harness) of one horse, he reached down to unhook the chain. Suddenly the horse jumped, and Otho grabbed the hame of the other horse and hung on for dear life as the spooked horses raced toward the barn. They stopped when they ran into the board fence next to the corn crib. Otho's father and older brothers came running. They helped him down and finished unhitching the horses. One of the rake's five–foot high iron wheels had hit a rock, putting a big bend in it. They continued to use the rake for several years even though the bent wheel gave them a bumpy ride.

One spring day Pop was plowing the garden when something broke on the plow. He asked Otho to hold the horse's bridle to keep it from walking away while he went to get tools. Otho was so small he had to reach high above his head, gripping the bridle as tightly as he could. Before long the horse lifted his head—and when he did, he lifted little Otho off his feet, still hanging onto the bridle. The horse soon put his head back down, and Otho could set his feet on the ground again. It seemed to him they were standing there a long time waiting for Pop to come back. Both he and the animal were getting restless. All at once the horse set his huge hoof down on top of Otho's little foot, and he couldn't move. He hollered and called as loud as he could until one of his brothers heard him and came running to get the horse to shift his weight off of Otho's foot. Otho looked down and saw blood oozing from his big toe. Since they were standing on freshly plowed ground, his foot had sunk into the soft dirt which protected it from more serious injury.

Otho and his brothers and sisters enjoyed riding the horses when they could, usually bareback, and loved to make them gallop. A brown stallion named Jim had a broad back and was calm and gentle. One time they decided to see how many of them could ride him at once. Seven climbed onto his back, but when the patient animal started moving, the child on the tail end slid down and pulled several of the others off, too.

Otho last worked horses the spring of 1948 when he was fourteen. He planted 120 acres of corn with two horses — Charlie and Bill. The weather was nice, and he planted corn from early in the morning to late in the evening, stopping at noon for lunch. It took him two weeks. His older brothers were working away from home during the week and came home Saturday night after Otho was in bed, sound asleep. They told him later he was driving horses in his sleep. They would shake Otho, and he would respond, "Giddy up, Charlie, Bill."

Pop sold the horses soon after that. By then they had tractors and had converted most of the horse-drawn equipment to be pulled by tractors. It was a sad day when Otho watched Charlie and Bill walk up onto the truck and go to auction.

But time changes things, as Otho would learn throughout his life. He had started life on a farm and thought he would always be a farmer. But God had other plans for him—plans Otho could never have imagined when he was a fourteen-year-old farm boy. Those early years had a purpose that would serve him well. He learned to be innovative in fixing things and in accomplishing tasks that often took more ingenuity and time than money, which they didn't have.

He worked on his father's farm for the next four years. Sometimes he worked for other farmers for a short time, but he didn't have a full-time job away from home until he was eighteen.

CHAPTER 2

A Relationship Begins

——

Both of Otho's parents were devoted Christians and took their family to Clear Spring Mennonite Church, which was within walking distance of their farm. It was established in 1810 and was part of the Franklin County Mennonite Conference, known today as the Washington–Franklin Mennonite Conference, and was among the most conservative of the Mennonite church conferences. During Otho's growing up years, his church discouraged its members from being involved in a local independent mission out of fear that liberal influences would infiltrate the church. In the 1960s, when several churches separated from the conference to become more involved in the community and in missions, his parents joined the new group.

The only times Otho remembers missing church services as a boy was when he was sick, which wasn't often. One Sunday morning when he was a little guy, he told his mother he wasn't feeling well. She felt his forehead and looked him over and said, "I think you can still go to church," so he did. He felt okay during Sunday School but began to feel worse while the minister was preaching. He jumped off his seat and hurried back through the center aisle to the back door. As he was pulling it open, he vomited — all over the door and floor. He hurried outside and straight up the road to home, all by himself. Otho's mother saw what happened and slipped out the side door with some of the baby's diapers and went around to the back door and cleaned up the mess. When Otho heard what she'd had to do, he felt bad for her.

Another Sunday Otho was sitting on the front bench with some of his friends and fell asleep during the sermon. He dreamed that he and his friends were taking turns jumping, and it was his turn. Otho jumped in his seat and almost fell off the church bench. Several people noticed and chuckled, including the preacher. Otho had no more trouble staying awake after that.

He enjoyed Sunday School, especially when Lydia Miller, Amos Miller, or Susie Eby taught him. They were all good storytellers and knew how to keep a small child riveted with the lesson's Bible story.

Otho credits one of his Sunday School teachers, David Eby, for helping him learn to read. David would have each child take a turn reading a verse of the Bible lesson. Otho wasn't a good reader and didn't like reading in public, but David wouldn't let any of them off the hook. Otho would count how many children would read before him and then count the verses to figure out which verse he would be reading. He'd read it over several times to himself before it was his turn to read it out loud.

When he was a little older, the bishop taught the young boys' class one Sunday. The boys were afraid to talk, so he asked them questions to get them to open up. Otho doesn't remember what passage they were studying but remembers one of the bishop's questions: "Is this passage just speaking to the people of that day, or is it speaking to us today?"

Otho answered, "Both them and us."

"No," the bishop answered, "it was just for them."

As Otho reflected on the class later, he thought, "That's why he doesn't promote missions."

Otho learned to take an interest in others from his parents who related to their neighbors and the community. His mother warmly welcomed neighbors into their home, which was always a beehive of activity. She would also serve food to the neighborhood boys who came home with Otho and his brothers after school.

She would often bake a cake–like snack they all enjoyed called cottage pudding, and would have it sitting on the kitchen table for her children to eat when they came home from school. They would cut a square from the pan, break it apart into a bowl, top it with fruit their mother had canned, and pour rich creamy milk from their Guernsey cows over it before digging in with a spoon. Then it was out to the barn to milk the cows and do all their other chores before supper. Sometimes the neighbor boys were with them and would enjoy eating the treat, too.

One day when Otho and his siblings arrived home, there was no cottage pudding waiting for them. Disappointed, they headed to the

The Horst family attended Clear Spring Mennonite Church, located on the corner of Route 68 and Ashton Road and within easy walking distance of their farm.

13

barn and did their evening chores. When they returned to the house, their mother was home and asked what they had done with the cake pans after they had eaten their snack.

"There wasn't any cottage pudding today," they told her.

It was puzzling. No one seemed to know what had happened to it. Several days later one of Otho's brothers found the empty cake pans sitting among the trees in the pasture field. The next time the neighbor boys came over, Otho's mother told them they had found the cake pans in the pasture between their house and the boys' house. They admitted to taking the treat. Without a word she served them more cottage pudding. While they were eating she told them that whenever they wanted more, they should ask. She would always be glad to give them some, but it wasn't right for them to steal. The cottage pudding never went missing after that. The neighbor boys respected Mrs. Horst and knew she meant what she said.

Otho's father was also active in welcoming neighbors into their home. He spent hours discussing Scripture with his friend, John Carbaugh, who went to Blairs Valley Church of God, as well as with other friends from the community who went to churches of other denominations. Otho enjoyed listening in on their conversations and learned a lot from them. It was the precursor of many similar conversations Otho would have in his life as he interacted with people from backgrounds and church traditions different from his own.

One particular instance of his father caring about the spiritual condition of others made an impression on Otho. On the way to church one Sunday morning, they stopped at East End Garage in Clear Spring to fill up with gas. Bunt was the attendant that day. Otho got out of the car to watch Bunt pump the gas into the car.

Pop said, "Bunt, you should be in church."

"Otho, I can't," replied Bunt. "I have to be here to sell gas so that fellows like you can go to church."

"If it means you can't go to church, I won't buy gas on Sunday again," Pop told Bunt, and he meant it. After that Pop always made sure they had enough gas in the car on Saturday to go to church the next day.

Otho's spiritual awakening came in January 1948 at a revival meeting led by Merle Eshleman. Each night at the end of the service, he invited those in attendance to accept Jesus Christ as their Savior. While the congregation sang a hymn, individuals stood to indicate their decision to follow Jesus. On Sunday night the hymn was, "Oh, Why Not Tonight?" They reached the last verse:

"Our blessed Lord refuses none
Who would to Him their souls unite;
Believe on Him, the work is done,
Be saved, oh, tonight."

Otho grew hot inside as he contemplated the words. He knew what he needed and wanted to do. He stood, indicating he believed in Jesus, trusted in Him as His Savior, and wanted to live for Him.

Several days later he realized a change had taken place inside him that was noticeable to others. He was in a garage in Clear Spring watching the mechanic Reed work on a car. Reed's wrench slipped and he cursed, as he often did. He looked at Otho and said, "I'm sorry, Otho, I didn't think about you standing there."

Otho was surprised. Reed had cursed around him many times before but had never apologized for it. Why did he this time? Did Reed know he had stood at the revival meetings? He didn't attend their church, and Otho was sure no one had told him. Otho looked down at himself. There was nothing different about him outwardly. Otho realized that when he decided to follow Jesus, Jesus started changing him inwardly. He wasn't obeying a different set of rules so he knew it couldn't be anything he had changed consciously. The only change he had made was to enter into a relationship with Jesus.

Some time later Otho spent several months milking cows for his father's friend John Carbaugh after John's wife Sarah died. One day while they were working, Otho complained to John about some of the ministers at church. "It doesn't matter what their topic or Scripture text is, they seem to always end up preaching about clothes and how some members dress."

"What do you think of Sam Eby?" John asked him.

"I really like Sam and enjoy his sermons," Otho answered, "but I don't like that he has to take turns with all the other preachers in the district and is only scheduled to preach once every several months."

"You carry your Bible to church, don't you?"

"No, no one else does," Otho admitted truthfully.

"Take your Bible," John advised, "and during the sermon, read the text the minister is preaching from and learn for yourself what it says. You'll get that much from the sermon, at least, and it may help you learn a lot more."

Samuel Eby, one of Otho's favorite ministers, and his wife Emma, who were also the parents of Otho's future wife Dorothy

And so Otho did. Church services became more meaningful to him after that as he realized the Bible text always had something meaningful to say to him even if the preacher didn't. It even seemed the ministers were preaching better as he focused more on what they said about the Scripture text than what they said about church rules.

Otho's appreciation for Scripture continued to grow as he studied it to learn more about Jesus with Whom he now enjoyed a close relationship — a relationship Otho would continue to rely on, cherish, and grow in for the rest of his life.

16

CHAPTER 3

Those Eight Little Words

Clear Spring, Maryland; 1951–1952

In the summer of 1951 when Otho was eighteen, Raymond Eby, the son of their late minister Samuel, approached Otho and asked him if he would milk their cows for a couple weeks. Raymond and his family were planning to spend time at his grandfather Moab Showalter's cottage at Sparkling Springs near Singers Glen, Virginia, while he recovered from cancer surgery. Otho gladly agreed.

After the Eby family returned home, Raymond thanked Otho and paid him twenty dollars for doing his chores. Then he asked, "What are you planning to do this winter?"

"I don't know yet," replied Otho. "I'll probably be helping at home."

"Well, if possible, I'd like you to work for me," Raymond told him. Otho wasn't sure what he wanted to do, so he didn't give a definite answer.

In September Glen Eby—another member of their church—was filling his silo when machinery they were using sparked a fire that burned his barn down. Pop and Otho went over to help him. While they were there, Glen asked Pop if Otho could work for him until his new barn was built. Pop agreed, and Otho worked for Glen for eight weeks.

One day while they were working, Glen asked Otho, "What are you planning to do this winter? After we're finished with the barn, I'd like you to keep working for me."

Because he hadn't yet made a definite decision, Otho was surprised to hear himself saying without hesitation, "I'm going to work for Raymond." The answer had come to him in that moment, and he was confident it was the right one.

Glen asked how much Raymond was going to pay him. Otho didn't know, and it made no difference to him. He

Lula and Raymond Eby

knew Raymond was fighting cancer and needed his help. Besides, Raymond had treated him as a friend and paid him fairly that summer. Otho wanted a job where he could help out and be a friend, not just a hired man.

Raymond stopped in at Glen's farm a day or so later. Glen mentioned to Raymond what Otho had said about working for him. Raymond found Otho and said, "I'm glad to hear you're planning to work for me. Can you start as soon you finish helping Glen with his barn?"

Otho agreed.

It wasn't long until Glen's new barn was finished, and they moved his cows into the new structure.

On the afternoon of November 5, 1951, Otho started working for Raymond and his wife Lula, who was Otho's first cousin. His pay was twenty–five dollars a week plus room and board.

While he was carrying his belongings into their house where he would stay, Raymond's mother Emma and his sister Dorothy arrived to help Raymond and Lula wrap beef to put in their freezer. Both greeted Otho warmly, grateful for his willingness to help Raymond and his family. Unbeknown to any of them at the time, Dorothy would become Otho's wife ten years later.

Raymond and Lula had four young children: Lucille (10), LaVonne (8), Karen (4), and Lynn (1). Otho enjoyed living with the Ebys and soon felt like a member of their family, playing with the children and enjoying conversations with Raymond and Lula in his free time.

The first winter Otho was with the Ebys, he named their cows. On his father's farm all the cows had names, and he was accustomed to calling them by name. For many of Raymond's cows, a name came to his mind immediately that seemed to fit the cow. For others, he couldn't think of any. So he wrote names on pieces of paper and put them in his cap. When he looked at a cow, he'd pull out a name. If it didn't seem to fit her, he'd pull out another until he had one that satisfied him.

As much as Otho enjoyed his time with the Eby family, it was also touched with sorrow as he watched Raymond's health decline.

At first Raymond and Otho worked side–by–side on the farm, but Raymond grew steadily weaker. In December he became too weak to go out to the barn every day. His illness progressed and eventually caused him to go blind, inhibiting him from helping with any of the farm work. He would tell Otho what he wanted to have done each day. If Otho had questions, he'd go into the house and ask Raymond.

Otho learned a number of farm management strategies from Raymond. He would have Otho stop the field work early enough each afternoon so he wouldn't need to rush around doing the barn chores and be late for supper, especially when they had evening plans. Otho also learned from Raymond to put straw bedding down for the cattle on Saturday afternoons and get hay and feed ready for Sunday. That way he had minimal work to do on Sunday mornings and could always get to church on time.

Although he wished the situation were different and Raymond would be well, Otho was grateful for the learning experience of taking full responsibility for the farm work since he fully expected to follow in his father's footsteps and be a farmer all his life.

He also learned much from Raymond and Lula about spiritual matters as he watched them live out their faith, especially in their suffering. One aspect in particular impacted him: no matter how much he suffered, Raymond never became bitter or angry with God.

One day Raymond was sitting at the table with his face cupped in his hands. When Otho asked him if he was in pain, Raymond opened his mouth to reveal many ulcers inside. Otho knew how painful just one mouth ulcer was. He knew Raymond had to be miserable, but Otho never heard him complain. In the years since when Otho has experienced physical pain of any kind, he has often thought of Raymond's endurance.

Raymond's health continued to deteriorate to the point that he was admitted to the hospital in the summer of 1952.

The sun had not yet peeked over the horizon when Otho walked down the stairs of the Eby home the morning of July 5, 1952, to find Lula in the kitchen.

"How's Raymond?" he asked, knowing she had spent the night with him at the hospital.

Tears slipped down her tired face. "Raymond left us last night."

Otho could find no words to say in response. Anger rose in him as he walked out the door to the barn. Normally he called the cows to come in for milking while he put feed in the troughs. By the time he

The Eby family—Lucille, LaVonne, Lula, Karen, Raymond, and Lynn

was finished, the cows would be there eating and ready to be milked. But that morning he was too enraged to call them. He poured feed in the troughs and walked out to the field to bring them in. Angry thoughts churned in his head as he strode along. He hardly noticed the pasture with its rocks and trees surrounding him. Suddenly he cried out bitterly to the empty field, "God, why did you take Raymond? His wife and children need him. Why didn't you take me?"

He didn't expect an answer. But as soon as the words left his mouth, a clear voice answered, *"Raymond's work is finished, but **I still have work for you to do**."*

No one was there. He was still surrounded only by the pasture and its rocks and trees. To this day Otho couldn't say if it was an audible voice he heard. But he had no doubt—in that moment or since—that it was God speaking to him. His anger and rage left immediately, and a great peace washed over him.

Those eight little words, "**I still have work for you to do**," became God's calling on his life and would inspire him from that moment on.

The evening after Raymond's funeral, Otho was in the barn doing the chores when Lula's brother Reuben came out to talk to him. Reuben leaned his elbows on a stall and watched him work. "Otho, would you be willing to stay and work for Lula?"

Otho didn't have to think about it twice. "Yes," he answered without hesitation. He continued to live in the Eby house with Lula and the children, keeping Raymond's farm going to support his family.

Others were also a big help to the family. The week after Raymond's funeral, a group of men from their church came with equipment to harvest his wheat. In just one day they completed work that would usually take a week— combining and trucking the wheat to the elevator and then baling and storing the straw.

Otho continued to grow spiritually during his time at the Ebys. He would often ask God for guidance when he wasn't sure how to proceed and Raymond was no longer there to ask. Otho's faith grew as God was faithful in answering those prayers, helping him to figure out what to do and how to do it.

Lula was also a great inspiration to Otho. He could talk to her about things he had never felt free to talk about with anyone else before. One morning soon after Raymond's passing as they were working together in the barn, Lula said to Otho, "The Bible says, 'In every thing give thanks.'" With tears in her eyes, she continued, "What are the ways we can give thanks in Raymond's death?" She and Otho thought of many things they were thankful for, including that Raymond was no longer suffering. Both felt at peace after recalling their blessings in the midst of their great loss.

In the winter of 1953, Lula decided to sell her cattle and farm equipment to pay off the farm mortgage. She asked Otho if he wanted to rent the farm from her. He agreed. He would continue living there with her and her children as he had for the past two years.

The bank wouldn't loan Otho money to buy farm equipment because he was only nineteen. So Amos Horst, his cousin and a minister at

Clear Spring Mennonite Church, helped him borrow thirty–five hundred dollars from an older man in the community.

Lula had an auction on March 19 to sell Raymond's cattle and farm equipment. Otho bought his tractor and other farm equipment and

Lula (center) with sister-in-law Dorothy Eby (left) and children—LaVonne, Lynn, Karen, and Lucille

tools. His life was shaping up nicely to become the farmer he had always dreamed of becoming.

EIGHT LITTLE WORDS

CHAPTER 4

Drafted!

Clear Spring, Maryland; 1951–1956

*D*uring and after World War II, the United States government required every American man to register with Selective Services at the time of their eighteenth birthday. But the peace churches, which include the Mennonite Church where Otho was a member, believe they should not participate in war. They hold a position of nonresistance and nonviolence based on Scripture passages such as Romans 12:19–21, which states, *"Dearly beloved, avenge not yourselves, but rather give place unto wrath: for it is written, Vengeance is mine; I will repay, saith the Lord. Therefore if thine enemy hunger, feed him; if he thirst, give him drink, for in so doing thou shalt heap coals of fire on his head. Be not overcome of evil, but overcome evil with good."*

The United States government honored this religious conviction by offering Conscientious Objector (CO) status and requiring them to serve two years in an approved humanitarian voluntary service assignment as an alternative to joining the military. Moses Horst, the bishop of Otho's church, helped young men as they turned eighteen to fill out their draft papers and ask for a CO classification.

When Otho turned eighteen in 1951, he requsted CO status and received a CO classification card. Later after he was working on Lula's farm, he was given a farm deferment (2–C classification)—a status he had to reapply for every year. Lula would request the deferment for him to farm for her since she was a widow living on a farm with no one else to do the farm work.

In the fall of 1954, Lula bought a house in Harrisonburg, Virginia, so the children could go to a Christian school. Otho's oldest brother Irvin, his wife Madalyn, and their children Richard, Ronald, Joann, and Rodney, rented Lula's house and Otho continued to live there with them while he rented the farm. He applied to renew his farm deferment in 1955, but since Lula was no longer living on the farm, he wondered if it would be renewed.

Over Easter vacation Otho and some of his siblings took their cousin Ruby Horst, a boarding student at Eastern Mennonite High School in Harrisonburg, Virginia, to see her parents in Arkansas.

Returning home late at night, Otho looked through his mail before going to bed. He had received a notice from the Draft Board stating they were giving him a 1–A classification (indicating availability for military service). This meant they had denied his farm deferment and could draft him into the United States military for military service. This concerned him since he shared his church's conviction about not participating in war.

Otho immediately appealed the 1–A classification and asked that his CO classification be reinstated, and it was. He was told he could request a hearing before the Draft Board to repeal the denial of his farm deferment.

His father accompanied him to the Washington County Courthouse in Hagerstown, Maryland, for the hearing. A secretary took them into a big room and told them to take a seat in one of the chairs around the large table. Not knowing which chairs to sit in, they stood inside the door. Finally a man entered the room and greeted them nervously. Several others soon followed. As they settled around the table,

Otho noticed they all seemed edgy. This was curious to him since it seemed he should be the one who was nervous, not the draft board.

The men asked him many questions. Eventually Otho and his father discovered why they were so uneasy.

One told them, "We know you want a farm deferment, but our superiors think we're giving too many farm deferments in Washington County. If at all possible, can you go into service now?"

"Well, I've planted my corn and have wheat I'll need to get in. If you give me a six–month deferment, I could go then," Otho replied.

"Okay, we can do that." They all nodded in agreement.

After the meeting was over, one man approached him. "If you sign up with your church mission agency for alternative service, you can choose where you go. If we send you, you'll have to stay in the State of Maryland in the 1–W program."

The 1–W program was established by the United States Congress in June 1951 when it passed the Universal Military Training and Service Act. It differed from Civilian Public Service in that it allowed conscientious objectors to perform alternative service overseas.

Otho knew if he went with the 1–W program in Maryland it would likely mean working in a hospital, which wasn't his preference. He was grateful for this man's advice. At the time, though, he didn't realize how much it would impact his life.

He and his father decided they would visit the Eastern Mennonite Missions (EMM) headquarters in Salunga, Pennsylvania, to see what service opportunities they had available. There they talked with Voluntary Service Director Raymond Charles. Raymond told them the only opening they had was in South Carolina where Otho's younger brother Daniel was serving in a hopsital.

"I've been there a couple times to visit my brother," Otho told him, "and I'd like to do something different."

Raymond recommended they check with Mennonite Central Committee (MCC) to see what openings they had. MCC is a Mennonite/Brethren in Christ joint agency that provides humanitarian relief.

Otho and his father left EMM's headquarters and drove to MCC's headquarters in Akron, Pennsylvania, where they talked to Orie Miller. Otho would come to know and appreciate Orie over the years.

He told them about the Pax (the Latin word for "Peace") Program started in 1951 by MCC and masterminded by Orie himself, a true visionary. The Pax Program matched the vast need of war refugees in post-war Europe with young Conscientious Objectors from peace churches who could build homes for them while fulfilling their country's draft requirement in alternative service. The first team arrived in Espelkamp, Germany, in April 1951 and lived in renovated gas munitions bunkers. Other teams did development work under the Pax Program in other European countries and South America.

Orie explained that MCC paid the Pax workers in Germany ten dollars a month plus room and board. The German builders kept track of the hours the Pax men worked on each house and gave the money they earned to the refugee family moving into the house to be used as a down payment on their new home.

Otho with his parents and siblings, taken three months before he left for Pax service: (standing) Mark, Dan, Ethel, Otho, Mary, Melvin, Martha, Elmer, Irvin; (seated) Otho S. (father), Anna (mother), Amos, Luke, Lois

The Pax Program appealed to Otho, and he signed up for two years in Germany. Since it was too cold to work there during the winter, MCC planned to send the next group of Pax men in the spring of 1956.

In MCC's acceptance letter dated September 2, 1955, Roger Haines gave him a general idea what his life would look like over the next two years: *"Your likely assignment will be building homes for Mennonite refugees in Germany. We now have four such Pax units in Germany— Enkenbach near Stuttgart, Wedel which is near Hamburg in the north, Backnang in the south, and Beilefeld near Hanover. During your two years there may be an opportunity to transfer to another area. We also have units in Austria and Greece in addition to men on special assignments in Holland and France."*

The Draft Board approved this plan, and the delay gave Otho time to harvest his crops that fall. He sold his farm machinery, Ford pickup truck, and cows in the fall of 1955. But Lula wouldn't let him sell his heifers. She told him she would raise them and their calves so he would have cows when he returned home and started farming again. He was grateful for her generous offer and consented. It was a bittersweet time for him. He loved farming but he also looked forward to the adventure of living and working overseas. He figured he had the rest of his life to farm after he came home.

In January and February 1956, Otho went to Eastern Mennonite College (EMC) for their six–week Short Term Bible School. He enjoyed studying the Bible, church history, and personal evangelism. It was his first experience staying in a dormitory. He spoke in public for the first when he gave the morning devotional after breakfast one morning. It was a great experience for him in preparing for the years ahead.

March 1956 was a busy month as he hauled several loads of his leftover corn to the Charleton Elevator, went to the doctor for vaccinations, and shopped and packed in anticipation of his departure.

He also spent time visiting people he wouldn't be able to see for the next two years. One significant visit was with Richard Oberholzer who had been one of the first Pax men in Germany. Otho enjoyed hearing his stories and seeing his photographic slides. He left that night with a better sense of where he would be living and working.

He enjoyed several long talks with his good friend D. Amos Horst. There were also gatherings with friends and family, including one his parents hosted and another at the home of his sister Martha and her husband Reuben for homemade ice cream.

On Sunday evening, March 11, after a typical large Sunday dinner with his entire family and a fun afternoon playing ball, Otho's older brother Elmer drove him to the Mennonite Central Committee's headquarters in Akron, Pennsylvania, for Pax School, the week–long training program for those going into Pax service.

Ten others were in Pax School with him: Herbert (Herb) Wiebe, Richard (Dick) Hess, John Hilbert, Allen Kauffman, James (Jim) Lambright, Harold Nissley, Herbert (Herb) Roth, Walter Schmucher, Paul Stuckey, and John Wenger. They all slept in the basement of the boys' dormitory.

The class schedule was rigorous, running from eight o'clock in the morning until nine o'clock at night.

On Saturday morning they tagged their baggage that MCC was sending to Germany for them. They went to Brook Lane Farm near Hagerstown, Maryland, that afternoon for a recreational outing. Since Hagerstown was so close to Clear Spring, Otho's brother Elmer met him there that evening and took Otho back to their home for the night

The next morning before church, Otho had breakfast with Lula and her children, who had moved back to Maryland. He ate Sunday dinner at his parents' house with the whole family — the last time they would all be together for another three years. That afternoon Otho said goodbye to Clear Spring, Maryland, his home for all of his twenty–three years. Along with his parents and brothers Elmer, Daniel, and Amos, Otho headed for Pennsylvania to spend the night with his Aunt Ruth.

On Monday morning, March 19, 1956, they left Aunt Ruth's for the twelve–hour drive to the harbor in Hoboken, New Jersey. Snow and ice covered the roads, and they saw large trucks sliding on the treacherous highways. But they journeyed on, arriving safely at the harbor where some of his family and friends had already gathered to see him off: sisters Ethel, Lois, and Martha; brother-in-law Reuben; niece and nephew Anna May and Benny; brother–in–law Alan; Lula, Lucille, and Lynn; and cousin Preacher Amos Horst and his wife Mary.

Otho's passport photo

Otho felt emotional as he boarded the ship *MS Seven Seas*, heading into the great unknown. Until he returned home, his only contact with these people so dear to him would be by mail. He was about to begin one of the most formative periods of his life — years he would later refer to as those he spent serving his country which drafted him, God who called him, and people whose needs drew him.

He had no way of fathoming in that moment the joys, challenges, and amazing experiences that lay ahead.

CHAPTER 5

"All Aboard!"

Hoboken, New Jersey, to Cologne, Germany; 1956

The ten young men who had attended Pax School with Otho were already on the *Seven Seas* when he boarded late on Monday night, March 19. Catching up and settling in took a while, and they finally went to bed at one o'clock. Otho drifted off to sleep to the sound of gentle waves and the slight bobbing of the ship.

Around four o'clock Otho woke when the ship started moving. He stared into the dark, his heart pumping with excitement and trepidation. He was truly on his way! Hoping to see the Statue of Liberty as they passed it, he got up and peered out the porthole, but darkness hid everything from view. He settled back into bed to catch more sleep before the sun came up.

It was cold and cloudy on Tuesday, the first full day of their trip across the Atlantic. Otho's weak stomach couldn't handle the motion of the waves. He went back to bed soon after lunch, got up for tea, then slept again until dinnertime.

Hoping that eating something would help him feel better, he went with the other Pax men to the dining room for dinner. He was picking at his food and trying to join in the conversation when nausea overcame him. Otho hurried from the room, but before reaching the door, vomited. A man sitting nearby looked at him with disgust. Otho was horrified to see that some of his vomit had landed on the man's coat. He apologized profusely and gave him fifty cents to get it cleaned. As soon as he could, he crawled into bed and stayed there until morning.

The time changed overnight, the first of six times in their eleven-day journey aboard the *Seven Seas*. Otho got up too late for breakfast but felt much better than the day before as his body adjusted to the constant movement. He enjoyed sitting on deck in the sunshine with his friends.

As the sun was sinking, they docked in Halifax, Nova Scotia, Canada, to take on more passengers. Otho watched with fascination as they loaded baggage into the ship with a large hoist.

The next morning Otho woke to endless miles of sea in every direction. They had left Halifax overnight. Tossing waves and a gray sky didn't make sitting on the deck appealing, so they stayed in their cabins most of the day.

On their first Sunday aboard, the Pax men congregated for a worship service in Room 503, where five of them were staying. Every other day they gathered for morning devotions together, either on deck or in one of their rooms.

The MS Seven Seas *which carried Otho from Hoboken, New Jersey, to Rotterdam, Netherlands from March 19 – 30, 1956*

Sometime during those first days, Otho pulled out the letter his sister Mary had given him with these words written on the envelope: *"Otho — don't open until after you leave port — but before you see the White Cliffs of Dover!"* As he read her letter, he realized the impact his going into Pax service had on those he was leaving behind. He was strengthened by her encouragement. She wrote:

> *Hi — you soldier (of the cross) —*
>
> *I couldn't go to sleep until I wrote a little love note.*
>
> *I can easily see why mothers, friends and loved ones hate to see their son (or loved one) leave for Army or Navy or whatever it may be, not knowing who their captain is, what type person he may be, where he'll take them (no port in view).... Thank God for our government which allow[s] our boys to serve God while they serve their country. Thank God for boys like you who are willing to give up all and follow him. Carry His banner high. We know that you didn't take this step for self desire or pleasure and that you didn't have an easy road preparing and leaving. But we do know this is the will of the Lord. Walk ye in it. Press on. Don't look back. Keep looking up.*
>
> *We know who your Captain is. You have an Aim and Port in view, so march on, Soldier, carrying your cross with a smile. We do not hate to see you go for we know we'll meet again. God bless you and keep you, God make his face to shine upon you and give you peace, joy and strength.*
>
> *I must close—sending my love and prayers with you. Read Joshua 1. You'll never be alone with Christ as your Companion. Where can you find a truer friend? Bon Voyage.*

Otho got out his Bible and opened it to Joshua 1. These words of encouragement scattered throughout the passage stood out to him: *"I will not fail thee, nor forsake thee.... Be strong and of a good courage.... Only be thou strong and very courageous.... Have not I commanded thee? Be strong and of a good courage; be not afraid, neither be thou dismayed: for the Lord thy God is with thee whithersoever thou goest.... only be strong and of a good courage."*

In the years to come while Otho was overseas, these verses would often come to his mind and strengthen him, giving him courage that God was with him wherever he was.

March 29 was the last full day on the ship and their first day seeing Europe. Otho and other curious passengers crowded on the deck as they docked at Southampton, England, and Le Harve, France, and watched several cars being unloaded from an opening in the center of the ship's deck. A big crane dropped a large cable into the hole and lifted the vehicles out one by one, swinging them across the water and setting them on the dock.

On Friday afternoon, March 30, the ship docked in Rotterdam, Netherlands. They had reached their destination!

Paul Ruth, director of Mennonite Travel Service (MTS), met the young men at the dock. It was wonderful for them to hear someone speaking English among all the Dutch chatter. Paul led them to the Pax unit Volkswagen vans where they met two of the Pax men they

When the ship docked briefly at Southampton, England, and Le Harve, France, a large crane lifted cars out of a hole in the deck of the shift, swung them out over the water, and set them down safely on the dock.

would be working with, Harold Muller and Merrith Hostetler. As they drove, Otho gazed at the scenes outside the vehicle's windows. He wanted to see everything he could. This was Europe, which he expected to be his home for two years.

They stopped at Hotel Schweizerhof in Koln (Cologne), Germany, for the night. Otho sank blissfully into the wonderful feather bed, tired from all the hubbub of the day. This farm boy was far from home. He had no idea then what the years ahead would hold but was eager to get started on his new life in Germany.

EIGHT LITTLE WORDS

CHAPTER 6

Pax Service, Germany

Germany; March–September, 1956

Energy was high among the Pax men the morning of Saturday, March 31. Otho and the others ate breakfast at their hotel in Koln before piling into cars to go to the Pax Center in Kaiserslautern, with plans for several sightseeing stops along the way.

Their first stop was the Koln Cathedral, the oldest cathedral in Germany. The impressive structure with beautiful stained glass windows was nothing like the plain brick building of Clear Spring Mennonite Church. Otho and the other Pax men drank it all in.

Then they were off to Bonn, the capital of West Germany, where they toured the senate building. They headed south from there, enjoying the view of the Rhine River running beside them. At Lorelei, the famous huge rock overlooking the Rhine River, they stopped to eat their lunch. Otho gazed in awe at God's handiwork displayed in the enormous rock looming above them. Their final stop before their destination was Rheinstein, an old castle along the Rhine River.

They arrived at the Pax Center in Kaiserslautern that afternoon. Otho was delighted to find letters from his mother and his sister Ethel

The Pax men and MCC workers enjoy an egg fry breakfast Easter morning.

waiting for him. They were his first communication from his family since leaving home.

The next day was Easter and Otho's first Sunday in Germany. He and the others from the Pax unit rose early and stood on the mountainside as the sun came up, celebrating their Savior's resurrection. After the sunrise service, they built a fire and fried eggs for breakfast before hiking back down the mountain to the Pax Center for a worship service.

Monday and Tuesday were full days as they attended the Germany Pax Program orientation, got their American dollars exchanged for German marks (one American dollar equaled four German marks), and visited the Enkenbach Pax Unit to see the building process.

The Pax unit leaders also interviewed each of the Pax men on Monday to best place them for the work they would be doing. They received their assignments the next day. Otho would be leaving for Backnang the next morning with five others: Dick Hess, Johnny Hiebert, Herbert Roth, Harold Nissley, and Walter Schmucker. After a month or so at Backnang, Otho, Harold, and Walter would move to Bielefeld.

By Thursday, April 4, Otho was settled in at Backnang and ready to begin working. His first work assignment was hauling blocks and mortar for the masons. Because his baggage from the ship hadn't yet arrived, he had to borrow work clothes from the other fellows.

The other members of the Backnang Pax Unit were Susan Kraln (matron), Canada; Honnelore Bregen (matron), Germany; David Peachey (unit leader), Pennsylvania; John Wyse (project foreman), Ohio; Carl Beryeler, Virginia; Wayne Epp, Nebraska; Ernest Geiser, Ohio; Merlin Gerber, Ohio; Johnny Hiebert, Kansas; Dick Hess, Pennsylvania; Harold Miller, Illinois; Harold Nissley, Pennsylvania; Herbert Roth, Ohio; Walter Schmucker, Ohio; Dale Short, Ohio; Mast Stoltzfus, Pennsylvania; and Roy Voth, Kansas.

Otho settled into life in Germany. It was his first experience being immersed in another culture and language. He sometimes tired of sitting through the German church services and Bible studies at Backnang Mennonite Church without being able to understand them. He took language classes so he could communicate at least a little with the German people. He and several others also sang in the German choir and interacted with the local youth.

One tradition of the German Pax units was visiting local families one evening each week. Otho enjoyed eating in their homes and hearing their stories — at least what he could understand or what was translated for him.

The Backnang Pax unit with a German boy "photobomber" in the background. Otho is first on the left in the middle row

Another new experience for Otho was attending church services of other denominations. While in Germany he attended Methodist, English Reformed, and Lutheran services besides the Mennonite services.

Otho saw firsthand the sad effect of World War II on the German people. In a letter to his parents, he wrote:

"I think Germany as a whole is dead spiritually. So we have a big responsibility to live a life that will be a witness to these people, and we really need your prayers as we go on in His work…. I think the war really put hatred in the hearts of most of the people. A lot of the people tell about coming from Russia, Poland, and East Germany.

We have been going to a German family's home one evening a week for supper and to visit. This past Friday evening two of the other fellows and I went to visit a widow. She has two girls, one 18 and the other 16; and two boys, one 15 and the other 13. This was a Mennonite family. Her husband was killed in the war. They lived in Poland, then they went to East Germany, then to Berlin and lived in a refugee camp, then they went to South America for seven years, then came back to West Germany in 1954 and lived south of here somewhere. About two months ago they moved here to one of the Pax houses. Her sister lives in Canada and she offered to pay their way to Canada, but she said she is tired of moving around so she isn't going."

Otho and the other Pax men worked hard at Backnang, building houses for Germans whose homes had been destroyed. Some buildings would house one family, and others, two. Otho's job varied from day to day, from helping the carpenters and plasterers to pouring concrete.

Every Friday was bath night. Since they didn't have showers in the Pax house, they trooped into town to shower at the public bathhouse.

In the evenings the Paxers often had picnics, sang with the local youth, or played basketball, softball, volleyball, or other games. On national holidays they would take the day off and go on a hike with the German young people or have a relaxing day at the unit house.

Several of the Pax fellows had motorcycles, and sometimes a group of them would take a drive through the country. Although Otho

Dale Short and Otho work on one of the German homes in Backnang.

didn't own one, he enjoyed borrowing others' motorcycles occasionally. Eventually he thought it would be nice to have his own. He wrote to Lula and asked her to send him money from his bank account.

By the time the money arrived, he had gotten pictures developed from his camera and discovered their quality wasn't good. Several of the fellows were buying new cameras. By buying several at a time, they could get a reduced price. Otho decided to get a new camera instead of a motorcycle. With the money left over, he bought a motorized bicycle from a Pax fellow who was going home. His purchases proved to be wise choices for the unexpected turn of events that lay ahead for him.

One warm Friday morning in early May, Otho and eight other Paxers loaded into a Volkswagen bus for a weekend visit to Holland.

Two more fellows joined them on their motorbikes. Otho was awed as they viewed acres of gorgeous tulips, saw picturesque windmills, and watched parades of floats full of colorful tulips. The farmer in him was also intrigued to see the massive dikes holding back the sea from the farmland that laid lower than sea level on the other side.

On Sunday they visited the English Reformed Church in Amsterdam and heard a sermon in English based on Romans 8:38–39: *"For I am persuaded, that neither death, nor life, nor angels, nor principalities, nor powers, nor things present, nor things to come, nor height, nor depth, nor any other creature shall be able to separate us from the love of God, which is in Christ Jesus our Lord."* The comforting thought came to Otho that even though three thousand miles separated him from home and his family, nothing separated him from God and His love.

They arrived back at their Pax unit in Backnang late Monday night. Otho unwound from the whirlwind trip over a cup of coffee and letters from home. Then he was off to bed for a few hours before rising early for another arduous workday hauling mortar and block. He was nearing the end of his time in Backnang. The next week he would be living and working in Bielefeld.

On May 12 Otho, Harold, and Walter left for Bielefeld. They stopped at the Children's Home in Bad Durkiem for lunch. There he saw Margaret Martin from his home community in Maryland. The men spent the night at the Enkenbach Pax Unit and attended church with them in the morning. It was Mother's Day, and Otho was many miles from his mother in Maryland, but right where God wanted him to be with her blessing. She had told him before he left for Germany that while she would rather have him living close to home, she wanted him to be where the Lord wanted him to be.

They arrived in Bielefeld that evening. Otho unpacked only the clothes he needed for work for the next day and went to bed.

Life and work in Bielefeld were similar to life in Backnang, building houses for the German refugees in the nearby development called "Bechterdissen." Otho's work was much the same as it had been in Backnang —hauling bricks and mortar. At both units they enjoyed the German "zweites Frühstück," a second breakfast around nine o'clock each workday when the matron brought

Otho works with other Pax men at Bechterdissen.

fresh homemade bread, apple butter, and hot coffee to their work site. The hard–working young men would devour the delicious food. Always slender before, Otho put on weight.

The others in the unit were Anne Driediger (matron), Canada; Fraulein Dick (matron), Germany; LaMar Reichert (unit leader), Indiana; Earl Schmidt, (project foreman), Canada; Merrith Hostetler (project foreman), Maryland; Dean Hartman, Indiana (later became project foreman, then unit leader); Allen Kauffman, Ohio; Jim Stemen, Indiana; Paul Stucky, Ohio; John Wenger, Iowa; Herb Wiebe, Canada; Harold Nissley, Pennsylvania; Marvin Musser, Pennsylvania; and Walter Schmucher, Ohio.

There was no Mennonite church in Bechterdissen, so they attended the Lutheran Church on Sunday mornings. The services were held in German and different in style than what Otho was used to, but he still

Otho hauls bricks for building new homes.

enjoyed them. One Sunday afternoon a month, the Mennonites held a German church service in the Lutheran church building, and he attended those services, too.

The Bechterdissen Pax Unit apointed Otho devotional chairman, making him responsible to appoint someone to give the devotional each morning.

On the Monday after Pentecost, a national holiday in Germany, Otho and Dean Hartman told the matron, Anne, that they would make dinner for the unit and give her the day off. They looked through the *Mennonite Community Cookbook* and decided on the recipe "Italian Spaghetti and Meatballs," knowing they could use canned beef from MCC for the meatballs. When they had the food on the table, everyone sat down to eat. Otho took his first bite. Something didn't taste right to him. He asked Anne what was wrong with it. She thought they'd used too much tomato sauce.

Otho and Dean warned the other fellows that if anyone complained they'd have to cook the next meal. But the only critic was Otho himself, who lamented in his diary that night, *"Until we were done the meatballs came apart. We used too much tomatoes, but no one has gotten sick yet!"*

One Sunday afternoon in May, over two months after he had last seen his family, Otho borrowed a motorbike and rode it out through the countryside, stopping on a wooded hill to read his Bible and write letters. Homesickness washed over him, making it difficult to concentrate. He began to pray out loud. It suddenly occurred to him he wasn't talking any louder to God in Germany than he did in Maryland. Otho was comforted knowing the Lord heard and saw him in Germany at the same time He heard and saw his family in Maryland, even though they were thousands of miles apart. In that moment the homesickness left him and never returned during his time in Pax.

At the Bechterdissen Pax Unit meeting on September 3, Orville Schmidt and Otho were chosen to go to London as representatives to the HPC–IFOR (Historic Peace Churches and International Fellowship of Reconciliation) Conference.

They left Bielefeld the morning of September 10 for London, taking four different modes of transportation (train, bus, boat, and subway) before arriving in London on September 11. Several of the topics covered during the conference were "World Needs," "The Changing World Situation," "The Problems of Young People and Service," and "The Suez Canal Problem Among the Nations."

In the Bechterdissen Pax Unit kitchen, Otho bakes cookies while fellow Pax worker Bill Maust samples them.

One speaker mentioned that one-third of the world's population has two-thirds of the world's wealth, and that one-third doesn't know how the other two-thirds lives. This stood out to Otho, even though he didn't know at the time how soon he would live with the other two–thirds.

Otho returned to Bechterdissen and continued to enjoy his life and work. Part of his responsibility in attending the conference was writing a report for MCC. He worked on it several evenings, writing it out by hand before typing several copies and sending it off to MCC. Unbeknown to him then, that report would serve an important role in ushering him into the next location and work God had for him.

In late September 1956, Otho went on a nine–day vacation traveling through the Scandinavian countries of Denmark, Sweden, and Norway with three other Pax fellows—Allen Kauffman, Jim Stemen, and John Wenger. They traveled in a small Volkswagen convertible, enjoying many sights during the day and sleeping in youth hostels or camping in haystacks, the woods, or the car at night. Otho snapped many pictures and never regretted spending the time and money to take the trip.

The Webb House in London, England, where Orville Schmidt and Otho were Pax representives at the HPC-IFOR Conference

Otho and his three Pax buddies camping along a country road as they travel through the Scandinavian countries on vacation.

They arrived back to their Pax unit in Bechterdissen on October 1 around seven thirty in the evening, ready to dive back into their work the next day. Fifteen minutes later, Otho had just settled down to enjoy a piece of cake and letters from home when the door opened. In walked his unit leader, Dean Hartman. With urgency in his voice, he told Otho he needed to talk to him.

Otho was completely unprepared for what was to come next.

CHAPTER 7

Nepal? Where's That?

Bechterdissen, Germany; September–October, 1956

Otho and Dean walked outside where they could talk privately. Dean took no time getting to the point.

"While you were away Dick Hess decided not to go to Nepal, and Dwight Wiebe called to request you go in his place. He's expecting you to call him at eight o'clock this evening."

It was a quarter to eight. Otho's head spun. He knew that at the MCC Peace Conference in Backnang in early August, MCC Executive Secretary Orie Miller had spoken with the Pax unit leaders about a request from the United Mission to Nepal (UMN). The UMN was providing medical services to this little country newly open to the western world and were asking for two Pax men to help them build three hospitals in Nepal. MCC had chosen two of Otho's Pax buddies, Earl Schmidt and Dick Hess, and now someone needed to take Dick's place. Otho later learned they chose him as a suitable candidate because of the report he had written about the HPC–IFOR Conference in London.

Since they didn't have a telephone at the unit house, Otho hurried to another house up the street and dialed the number Dean had given him for Germany Pax Director Dwight Wiebe. When Dwight answered Otho asked the most pressing question on his mind: "Where is Nepal?"

Rather than trying to explain it to him, Dwight suggested, "How about you go back down to the unit house and get a map and see where it's at and then call me back in an hour to give me your answer?"

Just one hour to process this surprising turn of events.

Back at the unit house, Otho found Nepal on the map and saw it was north of India. All the while he was thinking, "There's no reason I can't go." Still, he wanted to be sure. Otho talked and prayed it over with Pastor J. P. Duerksen, the Pax Pastor who spent time with each unit giving spiritual encouragement. Otho always appreciated him, his sermons, and the time he spent with the fellows. He was so grateful Pastor Duerksen was at their unit that weekend.

When he called Dwight Wiebe back at nine o'clock, Otho told him he was interested but wanted to know more.

"All right," Dwight said, "get on the train tomorrow morning and go to Amsterdam. The MCC director for Germany, D.C. Kauffman,

Pastor Duerksen (standing far right in front row) with the Bechterdissen Pax Unit. Otho is in the second row from the back, third from the right.

is there, but he's leaving later in the day for the States. He can tell you more about it."

The next morning Otho got up early and traveled to Amsterdam. What he learned intrigued him. By the end of the day Otho told Mr. Kauffman he would like to go. First, though, he wanted to clear it with his parents, especially since going to Nepal would extend his Pax service from two years to three years. That day while still in Amsterdam, Otho wrote them a letter explaining the situation. He concluded:

"As far as I can see now, I think it is the Lord's Will for me to go, but before I tell them for sure I want to know what you all think about it. I will have to stay one year longer. That will mean 2 ½ years before I'll get home again. There is one other boy going. We will be building three hospitals. We are to kinda lead it and show the people there how to do the building and also help some with the Missionaries. That is about all I know about it and that is about all anyone else knows that I talked to. There is another fellow there now, so there will be three of us. They had asked another boy to go, but he decided not to, so now they want me to go. They want to know as soon as they can, so they can get a Visa. They want us to go next month. So write back right away so I can let them know for sure. Pray for me that I will be in the Lord's Will. He has promised in His Word that He will be with us and lead us in His Will. I want to try to do my best in His Work wherever he wants me to be. I will try to answer your letter when I get back to the Unit. As the song goes, 'I want my life to tell for Jesus.'"

The next day, October 3, before Otho's letter could make its way from Germany to Maryland, someone from MCC headquarters in Akron, Pennsylvania, called Pop and talked with him about Otho going to Nepal. Otho's mother had just written him her weekly letter but hadn't mailed it yet. She sat down and added a P.S.— *"Well, I didn't get my letter mailed yesterday. Just forgot it. I guess it was to be that way. We got your letter yesterday and Papa also got a telephone call from MCC yesterday about you going to that other country. They want him to come down and talk it over with them. So I guess he and Amos will go down today. If you feel it is the Lord's will and they want you to go, I believe that is what you should do. I was looking forward to you coming home in two years but missionaries stay longer than three years so I guess we can wait three years to see you again or it will be two and a half I guess. I will write or Papa can write and tell you what they make out today."*

When Otho received his Mother's letter, he hadn't yet received official word from MCC that he was going to Nepal. But her letter confirmed his parents' consent, and he was grateful.

On October 15 Otho wrote to his parents: *"It isn't that I want to go [to Nepal], but I feel it is the calling of the Lord, and I can't seem to find any reason for not going, unless it would be for some selfish reason. I have been doing more traveling than I ever planned on doing, and I have a lot ahead of me yet. But through all this traveling I haven't found the place yet that I like better than CLEAR SPRING, MARYLAND."*

And so Otho decided. Less than two weeks later, on Sunday, October 28, 1956, he would be on his way to Nepal.

CHAPTER 8

From Germany to Nepal

Bechterdissen, Germany to Tansen, Nepal;
October–November, 1956

The next two weeks were busy as Otho prepared to leave for Nepal. He visited the doctor several times for cholera and typhus shots, worked on getting a visa to travel through India, and continued his construction work with the other Pax men.

Earl Schmidt, the Pax fellow from British Columbia, Canada, who would be going to Nepal with Otho, arrived in Bechterdissen on Friday evening, October 26. Otho and Earl went to the doctor the next morning for their final shots. By afternoon Otho started shivering—an apparent reaction to the vaccination. He crawled into bed to get warm. Several of the other Pax men piled six covers on him and put a hot water bottle at his feet. He finally warmed up and fell asleep.

Otho woke the day of their departure, October 28, feeling much better. After breakfast he and Earl said, "Auf Wiedersehen" (German for "goodbye") to the Pax unit and the Germans who had become their friends. They boarded the train at Kassel shortly after noon. They met John Hostetler of MCC at Frankfurt, who furnished them with one hundred dollars for traveling expenses, and Pax Director Dwight Wiebe at Heidelburg, who gave them each a box of candy and eighty marks to pay for their train tickets from Kassel to Basel. They continued traveling all night through Switzerland, glimpsing snow on the Swiss Alps as the clickety–clack of the train's wheels reminded them they were getting closer and closer to their new lives in Nepal.

They crossed the Italian border early Monday morning and arrived in Genoa. Before checking into a hotel, Otho and Earl found the ship agency office and bought their tickets to Bombay for the following day. Otho was looking forward to voyaging through the Suez Canal by ship.

Exactly seven months after Otho disembarked from the *MS Seven Seas* at Rotterdam, Holland, they boarded their ship in Genoa, Italy. Because the sea was so rough, Otho and Earl took anti–nausea pills to avoid seasickness.

They met the Paul Miller family on board. They were Mennonite missionaries returning to central India. That evening Otho and Earl ate their first spicy hot curry meal. The Miller family sat at a table close to theirs. Their children couldn't contain their laughter as they watched the two young men reach for their water glasses over and over and for their handkerchiefs to mop the sweat rolling down their faces.

On Wednesday morning they stopped at Naples, Italy. Otho, Earl, and the Millers left the ship to do sightseeing, including an intriguing tour of Pompeii — the city buried when the volcano Vesuvius erupted in 79 AD. Pompeii was rediscovered almost seventeen hundred years later, preserved by the volcanic ash that had buried it.

The ship was scheduled to leave port at ten o'clock Wednesday night but was postponed until eight o'clock the next morning. By then it was announced they would sail at noon; at noon they promised to leave at four o'clock; at four o'clock they claimed it would be eight o'clock. Finally, at seven o'clock they announced they wouldn't be leaving at all. The missionaries weren't entirely surprised by this disappointing turn of events. Earl had a radio, and while traveling through Europe, they had been hearing about Israel's invasion of Egypt, and Egypt sinking ships in the Suez Canal to block it.

The next morning they deboarded. Earl and the Miller family got their tickets refunded, but the office ran out of money and closed before they could reimburse Otho for his. He was grateful that later that afternoon the office reopened, and he received his money, too. They checked into the Hotel Santa Lucia in Naples, Italy, and their luggage was brought from the ship.

On Saturday Paul Miller reached Paul Ruth by phone and told them to stay in Naples until Monday, giving him time to make alternative traveling arrangements for them. The delay also gave them the opportunity to do additional sightseeing and to attend a Swiss church on Sunday evening.

When Paul Miller called Paul Ruth on Sunday, he still hadn't been able to make their traveling arrangements. He thought perhaps he could get air passage for Otho and Earl to leave the following day and would call that evening if successful. But evening came and went and there was no phone call. They listened to the news on the radio and heard the Canal was still closed.

On Tuesday afternoon they managed, with some difficulty, to get their luggage sent to Genoa where it would be put on a boat to Bombay, India. That evening Paul Ruth finally called. He had acquired air tickets for them to fly out of Rome the next evening to Bombay.

One more complication was to face them the following day before they left on the late morning train for Rome. After breakfast they picked up the paperwork needed to retrieve their baggage once they made it to Bombay, but the money Paul Ruth had sent for Otho and Earl to pay for the plane tickets hadn't arrived. It was resolved by Paul Miller paying for part of their plane tickets from Rome to Bombay.

Otho experienced his first plane ride when they flew out of Rome at ten thirty that night. A three-hour layover in Athens was scheduled for the middle of the night to assure they would fly over Turkey during daylight hours. Otho discovered he enjoyed flying and wanted to take a picture of the plane that gave him his first flight. But both locations where they landed during daylight hours — Basra (located on the Shatt al-Arab River in southern Iraq between Kuwait and Iran) and Dhahran, Saudi Arabia — prohibited them from taking photos. He was disappointed. They flew on through the night, arriving in Bombay at two o'clock in the morning on Friday, November 9.

After going through customs in Bombay, they got to the Salvation Army guest house at five thirty in the morning. Otho took a shower, wrote in his diary, and finally crawled into bed at seven o'clock. Breakfast at eight thirty came all too soon.

Their plane left that evening at nine o'clock, arriving in Calcutta almost four hours later where they met Edward Benedict, MCC field representative in India, and Rudy Friesen, MCC worker in Nepal, and stayed with them at the Bible House.

On Saturday morning they shopped for necessary items and visited the Nepali Consulate to get their visas.

They saw the Prime Minister of India, Jawaharlal Nehru, at a crowded public event that afternoon. Under the direction of his mentor

Drs. Robert and Bethel Fleming served with United Missions to Nepal in Kathmandu, the capital of Nepal.

Ghandi, Nehru was an influential leader in the Indian independence movement and was India's first prime minister, respected and admired by the Indian people.

Otho and Earl spent Sunday attending the Mennonite service in the morning and sightseeing in Calcutta that afternoon. Otho enjoyed the Young Men's Christian Service (YMCS) meeting that evening. It was wonderful to hear English singing and preaching again.

Monday, November 12, started bright and early as they took a bus to the airport to catch their plane to Kathmandu, the capital of Nepal. Otho first set foot on Nepali soil at a quarter after eleven that morning. Otho and Earl went through Nepali customs, then caught a taxi to the hospital. There they were introduced to ornithologist Dr. Robert Fleming and his physician wife, Dr. Bethel Fleming. Otho would soon learn that the Flemings were key to starting the work in Tansen where he and Earl would help to build a hospital. He also met Dr. Ed Miller and his wife Dr. Elizabeth Miller.

For the rest of the week, Otho and Earl did various odd jobs for the missionaries and hospital in Kathmandu, including painting three flights of stairs and various pieces of furniture and installing stoves for the Flemings and Millers. They also got visas that would enable them to leave or enter Nepal at will. A party with the Millers Saturday evening wrapped up their time in Kathmandu.

Otho and Earl left Kathmandu by plane on November 18, landing in Pokhara mid–morning. They walked the three miles from the airport to the Pokhara hospital with two older Nepali ladies carrying their baggage, which weighed an impressive eighty five pounds each.

This introduced Otho and Earl to coolies, Nepalis from the lowest castes relegated to menial work, such as transporting luggage for travelers or building supplies for the hospital. It was difficult for Otho and Earl to allow the ladies to carry their heavy bags, but they also realized it was how they earned money to support their families.

The Pokhara hospital where they stayed that night was located at a nice spot along the river with snow–capped mountains to the north.

Otho and Earl fly into Pokhara. The only means of traveling the forty-five miles from here to their new home, Tansen, is by foot through the mountains.

The full moon made the night without electricity not quite so dark. Using lanterns reminded Otho of how they'd lived at home ten years earlier, before the old red brick farmhouse was wired for electricity.

Now their final destination and their new home, the small town of Tansen nestled at the foot of the Himalayan mountains, was only forty–five miles away. But the only means of traversing the mountainous terrain from Pokhara to Tansen was by foot. It would take them three days to hike there, but they were up to the challenge.

Otho and Earl were up early Monday morning to begin their trek on the mountainous trails of Nepal — the first of many. Walking with them were two missionary ladies from Kathmandu who were also on their way to Tansen and three coolies who carried their luggage. It was a little warm, but otherwise a pleasant day for hiking. When evening came they stopped at a house for the night. It was a typical Nepali mud home with just one room, a dirt floor, a stove made of clay built into the floor, and straw straw mattresses for beds.

Otho and Earl sat on the floor to eat the rice prepared by their host, using their own dishes. Then they laid out their bedrolls on the floor and went to sleep.

Up at a quarter after five, they ate their breakfast, washed in the river, and were on the trail shortly after seven o'clock. Partway through the twenty–mile valley, the trail led them to the river. They quickly learned the Nepali method for crossing rivers — wading through them. Few rivers in Nepal had bridges.

The coolies lagged for most of the day. They would trudge along for about twenty minutes and then stop and rest. Concerned about their luggage, Otho and Earl walked with them while the two missionary ladies walked on ahead. They caught up with the women late afternoon near the foot of the mountains and decided to stop for the night. The two men washed in the river before eating supper and going to bed, again sleeping on their bedrolls stretched out on straw mats on the floor of a one–room house. The host family slept in their bed in the corner of the room.

The four missionaries woke early Wednesday to another nice day and were on the trail by eight o'clock, staying together most of the forenoon. After lunch Otho, Earl, and the ladies hiked ahead of the coolies. After a while the two women forged ahead over the top of the

Starting out on the trail from Pokhara to Tansen, Earl follows behind the coolies carrying their luggage.

mountain. Otho and Earl went around the side of the mountain and didn't see the women or the coolies until mid-afternoon. They ate supper and slept in another Nepali home that night.

Otho woke at four thirty. It was November 22, 1956. Back home in Maryland his family was celebrating Thanksgiving. He laid there anticipating what was ahead, knowing this was the day he would arrive in Tansen, his home for the next two-and-a-half years.

After breakfast they hit the trail by seven o'clock. They crossed two small mountains and started up the last big mountain just north of Tansen. By mid-morning their energy from breakfast had worn off and they stopped for an early lunch. Then it was on across the top of the mountain for the final leg of their journey.

They arrived in Tansen at one o'clock. Otho and Earl's journey from Germany to Tansen had finally ended. The two travel-weary men had been traveling for almost a month.

During a second lunch, they met the other missionaries in Tansen. Then Otho enjoyed a hot bath and shave, which were quite welcome after several days on the trail.

After one particularly steep climb, Earl (far right) rests on the trail with the Nepali coolies.

Otho looks down on the mountainous trail between Pokhara and Tansen.

The missionary women prepared a delicious traditional American Thanksgiving meal that evening. Otho savored the pumpkin pie and coffee served afterward when all the missionary workers gathered together to sing Thanksgiving hymns and have a short worship service.

Then Otho and Earl were shown where they would sleep. It was a room in the main hospital building used for both storage and church services. The kitchen was through a doorway at one end with only a curtain for privacy. The intention was that another place would soon be rented for them. When the two men later went to look at places to rent, they decided they preferred their improvised accommodations with its proximity to the others.

An exhausted Otho was grateful to crawl into his new bed by nine thirty. As he drifted off to sleep, he thought about how different life in Tansen was going to be from life in Maryland and from his months spent in Germany. The three–day journey walking from Pokhara to

Tansen and staying in local homes had initiated him to the Nepali countryside and its people. The warm welcome from the other missionaries when they arrived and the camaraderie they shared celebrating Thanksgiving together gave him a foreshadowing of the great times to come while working and living with them.

Tansen and its residents would soon occupy a special place in Otho's heart. He couldn't have known then how much he would come to love Tansen and all the people he would learn to know.

CHAPTER 9

Getting Acquainted

Tansen, Nepal; November 1956

Otho was grateful his arrival in Tansen landed on a holiday just before a weekend. It gave him the opportunity to get to know the other missionaries already settled and working there. They would soon become like family to him.

Unlike in Germany where most of his fellow missionaries were from the United States or Canada, here they were from various parts of the world, including England, Sweden, and Norway. Little did he know then how much he'd enjoy participating in the customs and traditions they brought from their countries of origin.

Also, unlike in Germany where his fellow missionaries were all Mennonites, the missionaries in Tansen represented a variety of Christian church denominations. His time with these dedicated people would deepen his respect and appreciation for churches different from his own, enriching his own faith and preparing him for the ministry and work God had for him when he returned to the States.

Dr. Carl and Betty Anne Friedericks and their children Richard, Anne, Chucky, and Jimmy were Presbyterians from Pennsylvania who had also served as missionaries in China and India. The Friederickses had begun the work in Tansen in 1954 and would continue living and working there until 1986. Carl was an energetic and adventurous man with a sparkle in his eye and a ready, warm smile for everyone. Betty Anne was a kind woman with a big heart, always interested in others. Otho quickly became friends with both—a friendship that would grow during his time in Nepal and last a lifetime. Their two oldest children, Richard and Anne, were often away at boarding school in India but spent enough time in Tansen that Otho became well acquainted with them as well as their younger brothers, Chucky and Jimmy.

In February 1955 **Ragnar (pronounced Rahg–ner) and Carna Elfgaard with their children Lillan and Lasse** joined the Friederickses. The Elfgaards were Baptists from Sweden. Ragnar, an ambitious and

The missionaries in Tansen when Otho and Earl arrived: (from left) Betty and Carl Friedericks with sons Richard and Jimmy, Ingeborg Skjervheim with Chucky Friedericks, Zena and Ieuan Timothy with their baby Jamile, Marjory Foyle with Anne Friedericks, Ragnar and Carna Elfgaard with their children Lasse and Lillan, Emma Eng

Carna Elfgaard at her clinic

hardworking go–getter, would be instrumental in the building of the new hospital complex. Carna was a nurse and midwife, a sweet gentle woman described many years later by her fellow missionaries as the ideal missionary woman. She opened a clinic in a nearby village where she treated small wounds and illnesses several times a week. Otho spent a lot of time with the Elfgaard family, growing to love and appreciate them.

Soon after the Elfgaards arrived in 1955, Carl and Carna set up a small hospital on the first floor of the house the Friederickses had rented. The Friederickses lived on the second story at one end, and the Elfgaards at the other.

In December 1955 Ragnar found land for the new hospital: a naked hill just outside Tansen which the Nepali people considered haunted. The government donated the land to them since no one else wanted it.

It was also in December that **Ingeborg Skjervheim**, a nurse and midwife from Norway, joined the team. She would come to be known as "Mother Theresa of Tansen" during her thirty–three years of service to the Nepali people. Years later Ingeborg's biography would describe the Nepalis' initial reaction to their medical work: *"There were many new things people in Tansen had to get used to. At the beginning they had no laboratory. When they eventually began taking blood samples, locals believed that doctors drank blood. And it was not easy for patients to understand why doctors were interested in such unclean things as urine and feces. But when the first X-ray machine was to be dedicated,*

Earl Schmidt and Otho

people stood in line to be 'photographed'" (Mirjam Bergh, *Ingeborg Skjervheim: Mother of Thousands,* 2009).

Dr. Marjory Foyle, a British doctor and psychiatrist, arrived in March 1956, bringing the medical staff at the little Tansen hospital to a grand total of two doctors and two nurses. She would serve the next thirty years as a medical missionary in India and Nepal, and at age ninety–three would be the chief guest at the sixtieth–anniversary celebration of Tansen hospital in 2014, speaking with passion about her time there.

In July 1956 **Ieuan and Zena Timothy with daughter Jamile** came from Wales to join the Tansen missionary team. Ieuan was an ordained minister and was in charge of their English church service.

Construction of the new hospital began in August 1956. Ragnar Elfgaard oversaw this work and had already struggled through much governmental red tape and lack of funding. But now, finally, the work had begun.

Emma Eng, a gentle, quiet Swedish lady, arrived November 8 to help in the hospital.

This was the eclectic group of missionaries in Tansen that Otho and Earl joined on November 22, 1956, adding their own American, Canadian, and Mennonite flavors to the mix. The team was glad to welcome these two strong and able–bodied Pax men who would lend a huge boost to the hospital building project.

CHAPTER 10

Introduction to Tansen

Tansen, Nepal; November 1956

*T*he morning after their arrival, Carl showed Otho and Earl his workshop in the front yard of the hospital. This was where Otho would spend most of his time during the first part of his years in Tansen. After lunch Carl took them out to see the land. "The land" was what the missionaries called the property located one mile out of town where the new hospital complex was being built. They also referred to it as "Bhusaldanda." Plans for the complex included a new

Tansen and Bhusaldanda sit at around 4500 feet on the side of Srinagar Danda (hill) which stands at 5000 feet. Otho took this photo after they had built a few of the buildings for the new hospital complex at Bhusaldanda.

hospital building, a new shop, a building called the "Godown" (Eastern Asian term for a warehouse or storage building), and homes for the missionaries.

The work was two-fold when Otho arrived: the medical services of the existing hospital in town and the building of the new hospital complex at Bhusaldanda. In those first weeks after their arrival, Earl went out to the land to help with the building while Otho spent most of his time in the shop at the existing hospital.

Otho soon became familiar with his new surroundings and the Nepali people. When he had left Germany, all he knew about Nepal was that it was a small country just north of India. But there was so much more to learn about it and its people.

Closed off from the rest of the world prior to 1951, Nepal opened its doors after the rule of the Rana regime ended and King Tribhuvan came to power. The new king invited foreigners to enter the country to help in its development.

The work in Tansen began after Dr. Carl and Betty Friedericks and Drs. Robert and Bethel Fleming, all missionaries in India at the time, visited Tansen for six weeks in the winter of 1951–1952 on a bird-watching expedition. During this time, Dr. Carl Friedericks and Dr. Bethel Fleming held medical clinics and cared for around two thousand patients. Soon after their visit, the people of Tansen asked them to return and build a hospital there.

The Friederickses moved to primitive Tansen in June 1954 to begin this pioneering work without the benefit of any modern conveniences, including vehicles, electricity, or running water. They hired coolies to carry every piece of furniture and equipment by foot from Butwal, sixteen miles away.

The Flemings simultaneously started providing medical services in Kathmandu. The work of these two families served to form United Mission to Nepal (UMN), which is still thriving today. It is an endeavor of people from various organizations, church denominations, and countries (nine nationalities and thirteen agencies when Otho

The original hospital building in Tansen also housed the missionaries. Otho's and Earl's room was on the second story, third window from the left.

was there). As stated on their website (umn.org.np/our-mission), their mission statement is: *"Inspired by the love and teachings of Jesus Christ, in partnership with the Christian community and others in Nepal and worldwide, we will serve the people of Nepal, particularly those who live in poverty: to pursue peace and justice for all; to address the root causes of poverty; and to make Christ known by word and life."*

The missionaries knew well the government's restrictions against teaching about Jesus in such a way as to cause someone to change their religion. Agreeing to abide by these restrictions was a requirement for entering the country and building hospitals. They understood they couldn't teach openly about Jesus, but would instead live out their faith in their everyday lives. This would prove effective in the years to come.

Tansen lies in the middle hills of Nepal and is built on the side of Srinagar Danda (hill) at an altitude of 4,593 feet. It is 150 miles west of Kathmandu (Nepal's capital), 45 miles southwest of Pokhara (the second largest city in Nepal), 50 miles north of Bhairawa (at Nepal's border with India and the closest location by air to Tansen), and 16 miles north of Butwal (the nearest town then accessible by motor vehicle).

The residents of Tansen were poor, living in houses without the modern conveniences of electricity, running water, telephones, or automobiles. Otho recorded in his diary the first time a wheeled vehicle made its way through the town. He and Earl crafted a wheelbarrow in the shop in early 1957 to use on the building site. When they pushed it out to the land, *"did the people ever look!"* Otho wrote in his diary.

He described the Nepali people in a letter to his family; *"They are brown and most of them are small and not very strong. Some live to be 70 or 80 years old, but I haven't seen very many that old. They have a lot of children. A lot die when they are babies. I heard once their lifespan is around 33 years old. I don't think as many babies die now as they used to."*

They married young, sometimes around age thirteen or fourteen. Arranged marriages were common, and sometimes the couple didn't meet each other until their wedding day. Otho's first encounter with such a wedding was less than a month after he arrived when the Elfgaards' fourteen–year-old servant married the garden boy. She didn't want to marry him because doing so made her a servant to her husband's parents, but her father said she had to.

Nepali girls being married to trees — a custom believed to guarantee fertility.

Just two days earlier Otho had learned of another custom when they observed the wedding ceremony of Newari girls to the bel fruit tree, a symbol of the god Vishnu. The Newar people were the original inhabitants of the Kathmandu Valley and surrounding areas. They believed this marriage ceremony for a pre–adolescent girl before marrying a man would ensure she would become and remain fertile, and that if her husband died, she would not be considered a widow.

They lived in constant superstition and fear of their many gods. One practice that shocked this dairy farmer from Maryland was their reverence for cows. As Hindus, they believed cows to be sacred and wouldn't eat beef or drink cow milk but would drink buffalo milk. Cows ran freely through the town and surrounding countryside and always had the right–of–way.

One day soon after Otho's arrival, he and a Nepali friend were walking along a narrow path and came upon a cow blocking their way. There was no room to walk around her, and she wasn't offering to budge. Otho did what he would have at home on the farm — gave the cow a gentle smack on the rump, and she moved out of their way.

His friend was frightened. "Never let anyone else see you do that! They would kill a man for that!"

Otho was sure to take note and never did it again.

Hinduism is the major religion in Nepal, with its caste system defining their occupations, dress, food, and way of life. There were a few of the lowest caste — the "untouchables"—who worked out on the land helping them to build. Later during Otho's time in Tansen, it was his job to pay the workers. When he paid the untouchables, they would cup their hands to receive their money as was their practice. That way the payee could toss it into their hands without having to make contact with them. But Otho would always place the money into their cupped hands, making sure to touch them as he did so. When they felt his touch, they would look up at him with big smiles on their faces. He wanted them to know they weren't untouchable to him, and that he valued them as much as he did the other workers.

Otho had to adjust to the Nepali food so different from his mother's cooking. He would often wipe sweat from his forehead and tears from his eyes while eating the spicy food. But his taste buds soon adjusted. About eight months later, he wrote to his parents, *"I'm at the place now that the rice and dal isn't good without any hot spices. Of course I can't eat it as hot as the Nepalis do. That is about all we eat when we are on the trail. We call it Nepali food."*

The rice and dal he was referring to was a common everyday dish the Nepalis made called "dal bhat," consisting of steamed rice (bhat) with a spicy sauce made from lentils (dal). They sometimes served it with a curry made with chicken or goat meat, potatoes, and vegetables. The agile Nepalis would squat to eat their meals, using their hands to deftly scoop the food from their plates which they placed on the floor between their feet.

Even though Otho came to enjoy Nepali food, he often missed his favorite foods from his mother's kitchen and garden—watermelon and cantaloupe, the cottage pudding she baked daily, the Red Haven peaches she canned each summer, homemade bread and butter with every meal, and her Swiss–German style of cooking potatoes and peas with milk and butter. In one letter he told his family about the sugar in Nepal: *"Yes, we have sugar here, right from the villages, with sticks, stones, and dirt with it. It isn't the nice, clean, fine white sugar that you can get in the store there. I'm used to that now, too."*

Otho and Earl ate their meals with the other missionary families. They would eat with one family for a couple months, then another family, and so on. Since most of the other missionaries were not Americans, Otho learned to eat and enjoy a wide variety of international dishes. He wrote in his diary one evening when he had just switched from eating with one family to another, *"I started eating my meals with Friedericks in the USA. I was eating in England with the Timothys."*

The climate in Nepal was also different from Maryland. Rather than four seasons like Otho knew at home, Nepal has wet and dry seasons. October through May is hot and dry. June through September

Earl and Otho eat their dal bhat Nepali style—scooping it up with their fingers.

brings rains almost every day, making the air cooler and more humid. Otho described it in a letter to home: *"During the dry season everything is so dry and bare, and life seems so dull, but there is a big difference when the rain comes. Then everything looks so green and lively. Even the animals look much better after they get enough to eat."*

Otho's first weekend gave him an idea what the church services would be like. At the time of his arrival, the missionaries hosted a service in Nepali on Saturday afternoons and a service in English on Sunday afternoons. Because they held these services at the hospital and were low key about inviting the Nepali workers to them, they fell within the guidelines of the government.

Partway through Otho's time in Tansen, they changed the English service to Sunday mornings and the Nepali service to Sunday afternoons.

Otho noted in his diary not long after his arrival that there were twenty-six children in the Nepali Sunday School (called such even though it was held on Saturday).

He wrote to his sister Martha on December 9: *"Our religious services are as follows: Nepali Prayer Meeting, Wednesday evening; Nepali Sunday School for the children, Saturday 12:00; Nepali Church Service, Saturday 4:00; Mennonite Hour Broadcast, Saturday evening 9:40, I try* to listen to it every Saturday evening; English Church Service, Sunday afternoon 4:00. I'm here finishing your letter, using my suitcase to write on and a kerosene lamp for a light to see."

Other than the church services, Sundays were often laid-back days, and Otho used them to rest, read books, or write letters. Sometimes he and his fellow missionaries played tennis or other games or hiked to areas just outside of town for picnics.

On Wednesday evenings the missionaries

Mr. John and his family

had Bible study and prayer together and took turns being in charge. Once a month they gathered at the Timothys' home for a prayer meeting. Everyone enjoyed those times of sharing and being together.

The first Saturday Otho was in Tansen, he accompanied Ragnar out to the land to pay the workers. The Nepali service was at four o'clock that afternoon, led by Mr. John, a Nepali who had become a Christian while living in India. The missionaries then gathered at the Elfgaards' for a party.

Later that evening he listened to the Mennonite Hour on Earl's radio. Although Otho's home church didn't allow its members to have radios, Earl's did. Ironically, it was a device forbidden by his church that allowed Otho to enjoy a reminder of it from the other side of the world. It made him nostalgic for home and all that was familiar there, and he wrote in his diary that night, *"It was wonderful to hear a service like I was used to at home."*

Otho spent his first Sunday reading and napping before the English church service at four thirty. A missionary from Kathmandu, Betty, was in charge and spoke on being a blessing to others.

The female missionaries took their turns along with the men in leading the services and preaching — a practice unheard of in Otho's home church. But he learned to appreciate each one and often noted in his diaries the insights shared by his fellow missionaries, men and women alike.

One song they sang often in their services was the English song, *"Oh happy day, oh happy day, when Jesus washed my sins away!"* translated into Nepali. Betty Friedericks had given the words to a local musician and asked him to make it into a Nepali song. He came back on Sunday to the worship service and brought several young men with him. The musician had translated the words into Nepali and used a Nepali tune. He sang a line, and the young men repeated it back to him. Betty was thrilled! They sang it often in their services, and everyone enjoyed it. For years after Otho returned home, he would often find himself humming the words:

Kushiko dihn ho, kushiko dihn ho,
djabba Ishu le mero,
djaba Ishu le mero paapa dhoe.
Un le sekaio, un ko ichanosaar, un lai prartna garno,
dinau aanan ma nai basau.
Kushiko dihn ho.

There were so many changes in such a short time for the farmer far from his home in Maryland. He willingly embraced them because of his desire to serve the Nepali people and soon adapted to his new hometown of Tansen.

EIGHT LITTLE WORDS

CHAPTER 11

Lots of Firsts

Tansen, Nepal; November 1956 – January 1957

Three days after his arrival in Tansen, Otho received his first mail in Nepal and the first from home in four weeks—a letter from his sister Mary and brother-in-law Alan. Letters were Otho's only means of communication with family and friends at home. He treasured each one even though the news was a couple weeks old. Some evenings when there was no new mail, he would re-read old letters.

Otho or one of the other missionaries would go up the hill to the Post Office every day. The postmaster was friendly and spoke English and enjoyed when they took time to talk. He was a stamp collector. Every once in a while, stamps were missing from their mail. They suspected he had removed them for his collection.

Otho recorded in his diaries when he received letters and from whom. One entry noted he'd gotten a "wonderful letter" from Amos E. Horst, his cousin who was also a minister at his church in Maryland. Although he received great spiritual support from his fellow missionaries, he also appreciated receiving spiritual encouragement from his minister from home.

The friendly postmaster poses in front of the Post Office in Tansen.

Toward the end of January, Otho received a letter from his sister Ethel, which *"sure left me in the air,"* he wrote in his diary. *"Your green Oldsmobile went to the junk,"* she had written, but said nothing about what had happened and whether his brother Melvin (who had bought the car from Otho before he left for Pax) was okay. It rattled him to realize something could happen to one of his family and he might not hear about it until weeks afterward. Sending a letter asking for details and then waiting for a reply could take a month. Fortunately for Otho, his mother had also sent a letter telling about the accident. He received it a few days later. Melvin had driven over the crest of a hill and collided head–on with a car in his lane that was attempting to pass another. The impact had bruised his chest, but other than that he was fine. It relieved Otho to know the rest of the story.

Otho was in Tansen less than a week when he noted in his diary, *"A woman died here in the Hospital last night."* It was a reality he would experience repeatedly while living and working with medical missionaries in a third world country. While many patients recovered, others didn't—a harsh reality for anyone involved in medical work, but even more so in a remote place such as Tansen, where equipment and supplies were far from state-of-the-art.

The hospital did have an x-ray machine and a darkroom to develop the x-rays. After several weeks in Tansen, Carl showed Otho one Saturday afternoon how to develop his black and white film. *"The first time I ever did it,"* he jotted in his diary. But not the last. He would develop many black and white photos in the hospital darkroom, often for the other missionaries, too. They sent their color film to Bombay to be developed.

His first shopping trip to the bazaar was to purchase a couple flashlight batteries and a mirror for their improvised room. The bazaar was a series of small shops, each carrying a specific selection of items. Discovering one with cloth and clothes, Otho later went back to have them measure him for a pair of pants which they sewed in the little room behind the shop. Another shop carried salt, and still another sold fruits and vegetables. Most prices were set much like American stores, unlike India where he had to barter. The bazaar also housed the post office and money exchanger, places Otho frequented more than the shops.

Shops in the Tansen bazaar

81

December came and with it Otho's first experience of the Christmas season away from home. The climate was different, the culture was different, the people he was celebrating with were different—all helping him to see Christmas in a whole new light that year. Living in the poor country of Nepal, Otho understood a little better what it must have been like when Jesus was born. He wrote his new insights in his diary, *"Living here helps me to understand more of God's Word, of how it was in those days, just what kind of stable it could have been. At home the stables are as nice or nicer than our rooms here. When we look at the ceiling, the white wash is coming off, there are cobwebs, and we have dirt floors with straw mats. The Nepali homes aren't white washed."*

Otho and Earl woke at five o'clock on December 13 when Ragnar, Carna, Lillan, and Emma came into their room with candles on their heads, bearing coffee and cake. Though the young men didn't especially relish waking at that early hour, they did enjoy experiencing the Swedish tradition of St. Lucia's Day, brought to them by the Elfgaards.

One afternoon he and Earl did some Christmas shopping. *"Quite different from home,"* he wrote in his diary. Other preparations included fixing the Friederickses' Christmas tree lights, making popcorn balls, and pulling taffy.

Several days before Christmas, the missionaries held a Christmas program on Saturday forenoon in Otho and Earl's room. Around seventy-five Nepali people came and heard the message of Jesus coming to earth as a baby. They put the young men's beds in the nurse's kitchen adjoining their room and used them for a stage. They seated the audience on the floor in their room. Mr. Timothy, Earl, and Otho were wise men and Otho sang the third verse of "We Three Kings" as a solo. It was the first program he had ever been in, and he wrote in his diary that it *"all worked out wonderful."*

The next day was Sunday, and the small group of missionaries had a Communion service with Mr. Timothy in charge. *"There were 9 of us,"* Otho jotted in his diary. *"The smallest group at any Communion I have ever been in."*

On Christmas Eve Carl, Betty, Marjory, Earl, and Otho went caroling to the Timothys', Mr. John's, and Yogan's (a teacher who spoke fluent English and taught the missionaries Nepali). On the way home they tried to take a shortcut but ended up in someone's garden. They found their way back to the house and sang for their neighbors, then had coffee and cake at the Elfgaards'. Otho and Earl wrapped their Christmas presents late that night before crawling into their beds past midnight. It had been a full evening.

They were up the next morning at seven o'clock to watch the Friedericks children unwrap their presents. After breakfast the missionaries gathered at the Friederickses' and exchanged gifts. Otho received a Nepali knife from the Elfgaards and one from the Friederickses, a Nepali cap from Marjory and Ingeborg, and a necktie from the Timothys. They shared a big meal of ham, wild hog meat, mashed potatoes and gravy, pickles, corn, soup, pumpkin pie, and apple pie. The house rang with conversation, laughter, and joy.

In keeping with the English custom of Boxing Day, they had another big meal the evening after Christmas—this one served in Otho and Earl's room. They pushed the beds against the wall and arranged tables in the middle of the floor. It was a fun night playing games and having a short devotional service together. *"This is quite a room,"* Otho observed in his diary that night. It was the only room in the building suitable for such gatherings, and he and Earl were happy to share it.

On the last day of 1956, Otho tabulated the letters he had written and received since leaving home on March 20 and recorded the totals in his diary: 145 cards and letters sent, 115 received.

That evening he and Earl hosted a little New Year's Eve party in their room with the single missionary women bringing coffee, cocoa, cake, and cookies. They closed out the year with a short devotional service and listened to Billy Graham's program, *The Hour of Decision*, over Ceylon Radio, a Christian radio station in Ceylon, south of India.

They welcomed 1957 with some good-natured fun. Otho crawled out of bed at a quarter after five, donned his overcoat and bedroom slippers, grabbed a cane Ragnar had given him, and stuck a pine branch on his head. As planned beforehand, he met Carl, Betty Anne, Marjory, and Ingeborg outside, and the group walked over to the Elfgaards' with tea and cake, wishing them a happy New Year. It was a gratifying "revenge" for St. Lucia's Day and they all enjoyed it, including the Elfgaards. Afterward Otho went back to his room and slipped under the covers for several more hours of sleep.

Since Otho had never read the Bible from beginning to end, he made it a goal for 1957. He drew a chart to mark off the chapters as he read them. Not long after he started, he decided to read some from both the Old and New Testaments each night, rather than just starting at the beginning of the Old Testament and reading straight through.

Otho delivered his first sermon on Sunday, January 6, 1957. Ragnar was in charge of the Sunday services and wanted each missionary to take a turn preaching. He had asked Otho to preach before, but Otho had declined. When Ragnar asked him again, Otho tried to get out of it a second time, but Ragnar wouldn't let him off the hook.

He titled his message, "In the Beginning, God," with the text from Genesis 1. Otho nervously began preaching to his fellow missionaries. About five minutes into his sermon, the door opened and ten Nepalis walked in. Unsure exactly what to do, Otho waited until they sat down and started again. Afterward he learned some of the Nepalis in attendance had never heard a Christian sermon before. One knew English well, and another was one of the most famous singers in Nepal. Otho prayed that the Word of God he shared that day spoke hope to them. After that experience Otho always took his turn. He never guessed then the benefit this experience would be to him years later when he would become a pastor.

The next evening the singer and about eighteen other Nepalis came to the hospital. Three of them played Nepali violins, one played a drum, one kept time with two small items in his hand that he clapped together, and one played the organ. They also sang several Nepali hymns. Afterward they all enjoyed visiting over tea and cake.

Two of the singers play their violins.

Two weeks into January, Otho and Earl had their first Nepali language lesson. Betty Anne Friedericks had asked Yogan to teach them Nepali using the materials that the Friederickses and the other missionaries had used. Otho and Earl told Yogan they would like to focus on the Nepali words for tools and building items. Yogan did a great job helping them communicate with the Nepali men hired to work on the new hospital.

Studying Nepali became part of their evening activities along with reading and playing games. Sometimes Otho took his Nepali book to the shop to study as he worked. The Nepali alphabet includes fifty letters, versus twenty-six in the English language.

During one language lesson, Yogan told them the story of a Tibetan who had never seen a mirror. One day he found a piece of broken mirror

Otho's language teacher, Yogan, with his wife and children

along the trail. He picked it up and peered at it and said, "Oh, I found my God. He has eyes that move." So he took it home and worshiped it. His wife couldn't figure out why he was doing so much puja (Hindu prayers) to this thing and spending so much time with it. So one day she looked at it. She said, "Oh, now I know! It is another woman." So they fought over it, but never with any resolution, because she always saw another woman in it, and he always saw what he thought was a god.

Otho observed to Yogan that it showed that people look for a living god to worship, not just a statue, and that he would like to introduce them to Jesus Who is a living God. After that he and Yogan would often talk about spiritual matters.

As Otho transitioned through all these first experiences in Tansen, it quickly became home and the varied group of people he worked with became family.

CHAPTER 12

Innovation Required

Tansen, Nepal; 1956–1957

During his first months in Tansen, Otho spent most of his working hours in the shop. He repaired, made, built, and even invented items for the building project, the other missionaries, the hospital, and the patients.

As a young boy growing up on a farm, Otho had learned early in life to use materials and tools he had on hand to make and fix things. Pop didn't always have the money needed to run to town to buy a new part or to hire a mechanic to work on his machinery, so he and his boys improvised by using items they already had on the farm. This skill came in handy when Otho got to Tansen where there were no local hardware stores to pick up bolts and nuts, no furniture stores to buy beds for the hospital, no medical supply stores to purchase crutches, and no prosthetists to order a leg for an amputee. Yes, Otho made all these things and more during his years in Nepal.

One of his first tasks after arriving in Tansen was making threaded rods to use in the walls of the new hospital to fasten the rafters down. It was a tedious, time-consuming job with only a small cutter to make the threads on the half-inch rods. Carl bought the rods in India and coolies carried them from Butwal to Tansen. Otho also fabricated the half–inch nuts for those rods out of a piece of half–inch thick flat-iron. He used a drill press to create the holes, a hand threading tool to cut the threads inside them, and a hacksaw to saw them into individual nuts. Filing the sharp corners completed the job. This would be a task he would repeat many times.

Otho saws flatiron into individual nuts with a hacksaw.

Dr. Carl Friedericks was also a man of many talents, and he and Otho would often put their heads together to figure out how to make or repair something. Carl had brought his hand and power tools to Tansen and set up the workshop. One they used often was his versatile Shopsmith. They could lay it down flat to use as a table saw or a wood lathe, or set it upright to use as a drill press. He also had a six–inch jointer they ran with a gasoline motor. Later, they purchased a bigger generator to use out on the land that could run an electric motor to power their tools. They also had a generator at the hospital to run the x–ray machine. They would some-times run a power cord from it down to the shop so they could use the electric power tools.

Since they used generators to run their electrical equipment, Otho and the others would take advantage of the times the generators were running to use the electricity for other functions—from practical tasks like shaving to entertainment purposes like watching movies, viewing their photographic slides, and listening to vinyl music records. Some of his diary entries described this multitasking: *"While Earl was drilling, I plugged my electric shaver in at the generator and shaved, then Carl shaved with it too. Earl shaved with his while I drilled."* And another time, *"Carl had the generator running, so I used my electric shaver to shave, and Earl, Ieuan, Carl and the cook used it too, the first time he ever shaved with an electric shaver."*

Each evening Otho would jot down in his diary a short recap of the work he had done that day, noting items he made or fixed for the building project, the hospital, patients, his fellow missionaries, and even toys for the children. These tasks required skills in carpentry, masonry, plumbing, electrical, welding, soldering, and engine repair (including gas, electric, and diesel).

He wrote in one entry about a "special job" he did that called for ingenuity: *"The one carpenter here that is a witch doctor asked me to fix his glasses, so I wired them together and put two pieces of wire on them so he can hook them over his ears."*

While Otho's varied skills served him well, some tasks challenged him as he pushed through to the solution and learned in the process. Several entries reveal that not all jobs went smoothly, and some caused him much frustration: *"Went out to the land to change carburetors on the motor, and I broke the gas line so I had to walk out and back three times and still don't have it fixed."*

But he persevered and another day was able to figure out what was wrong and fix it: *"Took the carburetor off the gas motor, and it was put together wrong so I took it apart and fixed it and put it on again, then I cleaned the air cleaner, then when I tried starting it again it ran fine, then I fixed the cap on the gas tank so it wouldn't leak gas."*

Another time it was the sterilizer for the hospital: *"I was working on the sterilizer, tightening it up."* And the next day again: *"I was tightening up the sterilizer and twisted one fitting off. Now I don't know how to get it out. I worked with it a good while this forenoon."* When it continued to defy him, he tried getting the pressure cooker to work so they could use it to sterilize items while he kept working on the sterilizer. But when he put gasket cement on the rubber of the pressure cooker, it wouldn't hold pressure. Several days later he wrote about the sterilizer again: *"I worked on the sterilizer this forenoon trying to take apart the*

Otho and Earl planing a board for one of their projects.

piece I broke. I couldn't get the pipe wrench to hold, so I was about to give it up. Then I asked the Lord to help me, and He did. The next time I tried the wrench held, and it came apart. Now it will have to be welded."

He worked on it again sometime later: *"I tried soldering the sterilizer, then I put it together again, but when I went to tighten that pipe the nipple in the jacket came loose again, so I took it all apart again."*

The generator motor also caused a challenge for him and Carl that spanned several days: *"Carl and I worked on the generator motor all day. We took the head off and cleaned it, but it still didn't run right, so we took it off again and here the intake valve seat was loose, so I took the valve out and notched the outside edge of the seat and put it all back together again. Started the motor and it ran fine. Carl and I were checking the voltage and all at once it stopped, dead as a hammer. Now it is tight. We can't turn it forward or backward.... Took some more of the motor apart today. The nut on the end of the crankshaft has bad threads. We think maybe that's what locked it. I tried putting it on the best I could with a pipe wrench and then put it all back together and started it and it ran good.... Finished putting the motor together and put it back in the motor room."*

Some tasks brought satisfaction, too: *"I did some electrical wiring for the generator so we can run the current through a switch box and also so that we can test it. This afternoon I went out to the land, hooked up the wiring, put fuel oil in the tank, checked to see that the fuel was going through all right and oiled the engine good. It is ready to go now."*

Otho learned to do things he'd never done before, such as his first concrete job — pouring a concrete foundation for the diesel engine in the powerhouse. He used a mixture of 1 – 2 – 4 and a lot of big stones and mixed it on a sheet of roofing tin.

He and Carl also learned to weld. After setting up the welder, they practiced with pieces of iron. Otho's first real welding job was repairing the sterilizer using bronze after his earlier attempt to solder it didn't hold. He wrote in his diary after finally succeeding in fixing the sterilizer: *"My first welding job. Of course it is a rough job, but I think it will hold this time."*

One nice day, Otho was fixing the operating table they'd carried just outside the shop door for him to work on when a group of children came in the gate. Then he saw two bears also come through the gate. Otho looked around to see what was going on before realizing a couple Indians had brought them to put on a show in front of the hospital.

Little faces would often peer through the doorway when Otho was working in the shop, watching in fascination as he handled the tools. Some would venture inside and search in the saw-dust on the floor to see what treasures they could find. The Nepali children had few toys and often played in the dirt. Their faces lit up when Otho gave

Nepali boys watch Otho at work.

91

them scraps of metal or wood. *"They really enjoyed that, almost as much as a small boy at home would a toy tractor or truck,"* he wrote to his family.

The most interesting and unusual item Otho made was an artificial wooden leg. After Dr. Fredericks had amputated a patient's leg below his knee, Otho had made crutches for him. But the man came back after several days and described how difficult it was for him to farm while hobbling around on crutches. Otho and Carl worked together to design a wooden leg. Otho took three–eighth inch rods to the blacksmith to flatten and make into two rings and four straight irons. He set up the Shopsmith on the porch to use as a wood lathe and turned down a piece of wood and fastened it to the iron. He

The artificial wooden leg Otho made with metal straps padded with leather

then took it to a shoemaker in town to put padded leather around the top to fasten it to the man's leg.

The man was delighted. He still needed to use one crutch, but now he had one hand free to do his work. Later, he became the chowkidar (watchman) at the hospital.

One of Otho's letters home described his work: *"I'm busy this week making a Hospital bed. Yes, this is really interesting work here. If they need something in the Hospital, they ask me to make it. Well, it takes me longer to decide what they really want and how they want it and how to make it than what it takes to make it. After it is made then*

they say, 'That is wonderful!', 'Did you make that?', 'How did you do it?', 'We need so and so other things made.' Well, maybe the things don't look too bad considering the person who makes them and the kind of material available. In the States they would turn up their noses at such things. Any way, they serve the purpose."

Otho's work in the shop brought him much satisfaction and fulfillment as it utilized his varied skills and served the people around him, making their lives and work easier.

His diaries contain many notations of a wide variety of items he made or repaired

Man with his new wooden leg

while in Tansen. This list is a small sampling of them:

- made a traction bed to hold both feet of a little boy
- sharpened a scythe for the garden boy
- fixed Emma's radio
- cut half-inch rods and threaded them for various tasks, including one to mount the diesel engine on logs and another to hold the framework of the wind generator tower
- fixed the x-ray machine
- cut glass for windows in the new buildings
- installed the glass in the Godown windows
- made a stand to hold sterilized items during surgeries

- fixed the winder on the tennis court net to hold the net tight
- built shelves for the library
- made a test tube holder for the hospital lab
- soldered the bottom of a thermos bottle for the Timothys
- made a splint for a little boy's arm
- put all the rods on the window of the first story of the Godown
- fixed the pump on the stove to sterilize water for the hospital
- made a sieve to sift dirt to make plaster for the walls
- cut rods for the x-ray room curtains
- fixed the microscope
- made a damper for the chimney of the Elfgaards' kitchen
- smoothed the bottom of two clothes irons
- built beds for the hospital
- made a dust pan to use in the shop and in his room
- bored out a pulley on the metal lathe to fit the new motor
- built an outhouse for the girls at the hospital, including digging a seven foot hole with the help of some of the workers
- made four small wooden wheels for Mr. John

Otho made these wooden tampers that he, Ragnar, and Earl used to pack down the dirt for the new tennis court beside the Godown.

CHAPTER 13

Farm Boy Turned Medical Assistant

Tansen, Nepal; 1956 – 1957

Before arriving in Tansen, Otho didn't think medical work was his cup of tea. He had chosen Pax rather than 1 – W for his alternative service partly because he preferred to not work in a hospital. Little did he know when he made that decision how much medical work he would assist with during his time of service — tasks he could never have done in a hospital in the States.

On the second Sunday after he arrived, a Nepali family brought a boy to the hospital who had gangrene in his hand. His whole hand and part of his arm had decayed. This case and others like it exemplified one reason Otho and his fellow missionaries were in Nepal: to bring western medicine to a country previously closed off to such services. It was the lack of medical knowledge that caused cases like this to become so horrifying before his family sought help for him.

Otho helped Dr. Marjory Foyle take an x–ray of the boy's arm. What she saw left her only one option. Otho assisted her while she surgically amputated his arm a little below the shoulder. *"It was aw-ful,"* he wrote in his diary of the experience. It was the first of several amputations he would watch or assist with during his time in Nepal. Awful as they were, both for the missionaries to perform and the patients to endure, Otho realized that in every case the choice to amputate was necessary to save the life of the patient.

Later that month he watched as one of the doctors grafted skin on the leg of a baby who had suffered burns.

In January they experienced torrential rains that caused much damage. A Nepali man had the misfortune of his house falling on him, covering him up to his neck and breaking his leg above the knee. Otho assisted Carl in setting up traction for him. Using a hand drill from the shop, Carl drilled a steel pin through the man's leg until the drill wouldn't hold any longer. Otho retrieved vice grips from the shop, and Carl used them to turn the pin through the leg. They used ten-pound sandbags for weights.

The next evening at the supper table, Carl mentioned he was planning to operate on a man that evening and needed someone to hold the light for him. Otho volunteered. When they got to the operating room, Carl explained the surgery was for a diabetic man whose leg had developed gangrene. To save his life, they needed to amputate. Otho's first task was to pour water over Carl, Marjory, and Ingeborg's hands for ten minutes while they scrubbed for surgery. He then put on a mask, along with the others, and watched as Carl cut through the leg just below his knee. Marjory clamped the vessels as Carl cut them, using fifteen to twenty clamps. After sawing through the two bones, Carl asked Otho to hold the patient's foot and keep his leg stretched so he could finish cutting through the rest of the flesh. He finished, and Otho stood there holding the detached leg.

"What should I do with it?" he asked Carl.

Carl turned to look at Otho and burst out laughing at the sight of him holding the leg. His laughter lightened the somber mood in the operating room. He told Otho to lay it on a newspaper on the

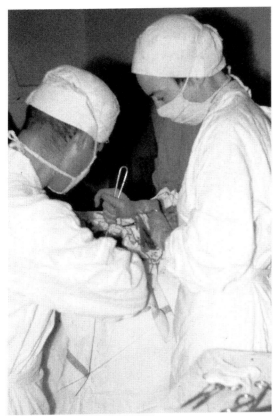

Dr. Friedericks and Dr. Foyle operate on a patient.

floor. Otho then watched while they tied off the clamped blood vessels with catgut. When they finished, he helped carry the man to the ward and put weights on his leg. Sadly, the man died ten days later. A hospital worker took his body down to the river and burned it—the Hindu method of disposing bodies.

Otho's task the next day in the hospital was to help set up traction for a little Nepali boy whose femur broke when a horse kicked him. A month later, Otho held a man's leg while Carl put a cast on it, and then sat with the patient until he awoke from anesthesia.

Carl asked Otho that same day to watch the screen of the x-ray machine while a man drank dye so they could observe the lining of his stomach. Another afternoon, Otho watched Carl x-ray four men who had Tuberculosis. Looking at the x-rays, he could see the effect of the disease. Otho found these tasks interesting even if he wasn't trained to understand everything he was seeing.

In April a little girl came to the hospital with gangrene progressed in her arm to the point they could see the bone. Otho came into the hospital just as they were ready to start the amputation, and Carl asked Otho to lead in prayer before he began surgery. Another day that month, Otho accompanied Carna after dark to a village to visit a patient.

That summer after they had moved the shop out to the land, Otho was asked to bring vise grips into the hospital in Tansen to pull a steel pin from the knee of a girl in traction. On another errand to the hospital to clean out the gas lines of the generator motor, Otho saw a man there who had been bitten while attempting to remove a snake's teeth.

Another snake bite he observed was more graphic. When Otho went to the hospital one day, a boy was sitting on the veranda who had been bitten a month before. Someone had tied his arm tight and gangrene developed up to his elbow. His hand was now black skin stretched over the bones, but between his elbow and wrist the flesh and skin had rotted away, and only two bones remained. Otho wrote in his diary, *"I have heard ... of someone being skin and bones, but that is the first I ever saw just the bones. They looked white, and all the flesh and skin was off."*

It was appalling to him. Better education and quicker treatment could have prevented the boy's condition from progressing to this dire state. But this is why they were in Nepal—to bring a better way of life to this primitive country.

In the Spring of 1958, Otho made an operating traction table per Carl's instructions. The plan was to fix the leg of a girl whose broken leg hadn't healed correctly. She had fallen out of a tree six weeks before, breaking her femur. The bones had lapped over, making her left leg two inches shorter than the right one. The day after Otho finished the table, he assisted with the three–hour operation. Carl cut her leg to the bone and then cut through the bone with a hammer and chisel. Otho tightened the traction until the leg was as long as the other one and watched as Carl made sure the two bones lined up before sewing her leg shut. Afterward, he put casts on both legs all the way to her waist so she couldn't move while her leg healed. Otho wrote to his parents, *"It was really interesting. Now I understand how they set [his brother] Mark's leg that time by cutting it."*

The traction table Otho made for Carl to operate on a girl whose broken leg had not healed properly. Later, he took it apart and made a card box stand out of it.

During church one Sunday, Marjory came in and asked Otho if he would come to the hospital and help her with a woman who had a broken back. He made a couple of foot splints for the woman and boards for under her back.

After Otho started working with the building project on the land, he wasn't at the hospital in Tansen as much. But that didn't end his medical aid to the Nepali people. Because of the workers' fierce loyalty, once Otho was overseeing their work, they would only go to him if they needed medical attention. In a letter to his parents on June 19, 1958, he wrote, *"Well, I had to stop and doctor one of my worker's legs. He was cutting stones and a piece of stone flew up and cut his leg a little. That is one thing about these people. They are really loyal to whoever they are working under. If they have a sore or pain or something they will always come to me. So the nurses fixed up a first-aid box for me to treat them. Last week one of our workers fell out of a tree at his house and broke his back. His friends told me about it, so I told them to take him to the Hospital. Two days later they brought him to me. I told them*

99

there was nothing I could do, they would have to take him on in to the Hospital. Before they would go, they wanted a note to give to the doctor from me. The poor boy, he usually carries things to Butwal for us when we go out, but now he won't be able to do anything for 6 months, and it will be a year or more before he can carry a big load to Butwal again."

One day a boy came and asked Otho to go with him to see a sick child. When they arrived at the house, Otho could see that the child, who was about two years old, was dead. His family didn't think he was, but Otho couldn't find a pulse or detect any breathing. They thought he should be able to do something. Otho felt helpless, especially since he didn't know enough Nepali to communicate well with them.

As he left the house, he went up to the main path where a Nepali man came to him with a goat and asked Otho what was wrong with it. The goat's nose was bleeding and it wouldn't eat. Again, he felt helpless as he didn't know what to do for it.

Another time a Nepali asked him to go look at a sick cow. As soon as Otho saw the cow, he could see she was bloated. As a dairy farmer, this was a medical condition he knew something about. He explained to them how to plunge a knife into her stomach to release the gas. They wanted Otho to do it, but he declined, knowing how sacred cows were to them and not knowing what they would do if he accidentally harmed the cow. No one else would do it, either. Sadly, the cow died several days later.

Although Otho had thought he wouldn't enjoy medical work, he discovered it to be fascinating even though it still wasn't his cup of tea. What was his cup of tea was serving the Nepali people in any way he could, and if that meant giving medical help, he was glad to do it. He was grateful to have these experiences and the opportunity to assist in saving Nepali lives and making their lives healthier and easier.

CHAPTER 14

Adventures of Everyday Life in Tansen

Tansen, Nepal; January–February, 1957

Otho quickly discovered that life was never dull in Tansen. On the second day of 1957, he went with Carl out to the land to sharpen the planer. When they arrived at ten thirty in the morning, none of the workers were there. The foreman had quit not long before and then decided he wanted to come back to work, but Ragnar and Carl wouldn't let him. In retaliation he tried to convince the other workers to quit, too. It appeared he had succeeded. But after a while they saw the men coming down over the hill to the building site. Their desire to keep their jobs had prevailed.

During the second week of January, the clouds that had been covering Tansen for several days gave way to torrential rains. It was the "Christmas rain," as they called it in that region of Nepal, but was late that year. The air turned cold as the rain fell day and night and the winds blew. Otho worked inside the shop most of the time and kept a little charcoal stove going to take off the chill. He worked by the light of a Petromax, a pressurized kerosene lamp. No one went out to the land because it was so wet and messy.

On Thursday the sun finally broke through the clouds. Otho, Earl, and Ragnar trekked out to the land to check on the new buildings, which were being built from unbaked mud bricks. When they got there, they all stood and stared at the awful scene before them. Half the Godown, which had been nearing completion, had fallen down. One of the window frames laid on the ground below its proper place. At least half of the building would need to be taken down and built again. The Elfgaards' house which had been almost ready for its roof had also lost its window frames. It, too, would need to be torn down and rebuilt.

Carl, Betty, and Richie came out while they were there to see what damage the rains had caused. Their house had just been started, the walls standing about three feet tall. It didn't take long to make an assessment: it, too, would need to be torn down and started over.

The stacked bricks were now just a pile of mud. Shoulders slumped and words wouldn't come. They had worked so hard, looking forward

Earl, Carl, Ragnar, Betty, and Richie observe the damage to the Friederickses house after the heavy rains.

Ragnar examines the damage to his house, which had been ready for the roof.

to moving out to the land and opening the hospital there as soon as they could. But they also realized this was just a setback. They would rebuild.

This time, though, they would purchase kiln–baked bricks for the outside layer of the two–foot thick outer walls so they wouldn't dissolve under the heavy rains. The workers would continue to make the sun–dried bricks for the inner part of the walls.

The downside of using the kiln–baked bricks, besides needing to purchase them, was that they needed to be carried from the valley below Tansen at 3,000 feet elevation to the land at 4,500 feet. They hired coolies to carry them. Otho would often see women and their children carrying the bricks up from the valley with the smallest of children carrying one or two bricks. The missionaries paid each person per brick carried, including the children who beamed when they received their pay.

Later during the rainy season from June through September, they were grateful they had already switched to using kiln–baked bricks. So much more of their work would have been destroyed if they continued using the sun–dried bricks for the outer walls. The late Christmas rain

Coolies, which included women and children, were hired to carry the kiln-dried bricks from the valley 1,500 feet below Bhusaldanda.

in January had been a blessing in disguise, causing them to switch earlier rather than later to the more durable kiln–baked bricks.

In the middle of January, Otho and Earl moved to the "attic," a little ten–by–ten foot room on the top floor of the United Mission Hospital. Planks laid over some of the joists created a low ceiling on part of the room and allowed for storage above it. Otho's head brushed against the planks when he stood upright, but Earl, at over six feet tall, could only stand up straight when he was in the middle of the room where there were no planks. The single window looked out over Tansen. Carna made curtains for their window and gave them two farm pictures to hang on their walls. Otho fixed up a box with shelves for clothes and put up a rack for coats, pants, and towels. Their two beds lined the walls with a desk in between. Otho put a board in the center of the desk drawer so Earl could use one side, and he the other.

Although they managed to fit everything into their tiny room, not all their belongings had arrived yet. After much paperwork and back and forth with the shipping company and the Indian customs to get them to Tansen, Earl's trunk and Otho's blue foot locker finally arrived on March 13. It was exactly four months from the day they had sent the luggage ahead of them from Genoa, Italy. Otho unpacked his belongings from his footlocker. Looking around their tiny room, he realized there was no space left to store the items. He packed them back into the locker except for some of his books. He was glad to have more of his work clothes, especially his work shoes. His feet had been getting sore without them.

Earl plays his trumpet outside the door to his and Otho's room at the Godown.

One evening Otho and Earl were each sitting on their beds reading by the light of the Petromax hanging on a stick. The heat from the lamp caused the stick to burn in two. The Petromax crashed to the floor, startling the two young men who didn't know at first what was happening. They cleaned up the mess and finished their reading and diary writing that night using flashlights. In the darkness they could see the cannon going off that announced the beginning of the curfew imposed by the town. Otho noted in his diary that *"it looked a lot like the fireworks going off at home, only it didn't go up in the air."*

The two Pax fellows got along well together. Soon after they moved into the attic room, Earl asked Otho if he would mind if he played his trumpet in their room.

"No, if you don't mind if I sing along," Otho told him.

Earl would stand facing the window playing his trumpet while Otho sang. They were usually songs they both knew, but sometimes Earl would make up tunes while Otho made up words and sang along. They later learned that on the other side of the thin wall in her own room, Mary Cundy would often sing along with them.

Otho enjoyed singing, whether by himself or with others. At home on the farm, he had often sung at the top of his lungs when driving the tractor, even as a young boy. When his brother Elmer got a guitar, he learned to play and was getting pretty good at it when Pop decided to milk three times a day. After that Otho no longer had time to practice. Now in Nepal, music was once again a favorite pastime for him. Some evenings when he was by himself, he would sing from the songbooks he had brought along. He noted in his diary one evening, *"I started to sing in the Brunk song book. Sang the first 17 songs this eve. Sometimes when I'm alone and am happy, I find nothing better to do than to sing*

The workers make sun-dried bricks for the inside walls of the new buildings.

some good Hymns and Gospel songs." And another time, *"After supper I sang for about an hour from the 'Church and Sunday School Hymnal,' alone here in my room."*

Another of Otho's evening activities was writing a report of his work in Tansen for MCC. After writing it out by hand, he would type four copies: one to send to MCC headquarters in Akron, one to send to Dwight Wiebe (Pax director in Germany), one to Edward Benedict (MCC director for India and Nepal), and one to keep for himself.

———————

As the rebuilding started up again out on the land after the devastating rains, Otho would go out to oversee the workers some days instead of working in the shop. Otho was grateful Yogan had taught him the Nepali names for the tools. He was better able to explain to the workers how the missionaries wanted things done.

One day Otho was trying to explain to the head mason, Kanooge, how to build the fireplace across the corner of the living room in one of the houses. They needed to taper the chimney up the wall to go out the roof. Kanooge had never built one like that before. Otho wasn't sure how to explain it to him, so he thought he would demonstrate. As he picked up the brick and reached for the mortar, Kanooge stopped him. Grabbing the brick out of Otho's hand, he started laying up the bricks on a taper, just as Otho intended. Otho was amazed Kanooge had understood and watched as he did a wonderful job.

The Nepalis often sang as they worked. They enjoyed singing a song Ragnar taught them, but added more words to it. One time Otho heard them making up a song about Jesus and their work on the hospital.

On the first day of February, Otho and Ragnar counted the sun-dried bricks the workers were making for the inner walls. There were 50,000 stacked and ready. The first floor of the Godown was completed, waiting for the second. Progress was finally being made.

Grateful for work to support their families, female coolies carry manure to be used in making the sun-dried bricks. Note the corner of the tennis court to the right of the Godown and the valley below.

To make the sun-dried bricks, women bring water to the mud workers who use their feet to mix it with dirt and manure.

CHAPTER 15

Moving Out to the Land

Tansen, Nepal; March–November 1957

On March 9 the Elfgaards moved from the hospital in Tansen to the second story of the now-finished Godown. Everything was carried by foot. Several days later, Carl bought a heavy 7.5 HP diesel motor and generator from their neighbor in town. It took all day to move it out to the land. Sixteen of the workers helped Otho and Carl carry it most of the way, and then Earl sent three more to help with the final distance. Carna had hot coffee ready for the tired crew after they finally had the generator in place. Otho soothed his aching muscles that night with a hot bath.

At the end of March, the missionaries held a dedication service for the Godown and served a meal to the workers. It bothered Otho to see the untouchables sittting separate from the other workers who wouldn't allow the untouchables to come near them while they were eating. After the meal Ragnar gave a message in English, interpreted for the Nepali workers, and they sang a few songs.

On their way back to Tansen, Otho and the others met Yogan. When they got to the Tundikhel (open parade ground), Surendra

The Nepali workers and missionaries gather for a dedication of the Godown, the first completed building of the new hospital complex.

and Sodemba (two Christian teachers from India), Yogan, and Otho walked around town for a while. They met Yoge the young school-teacher and he asked them to sing for him. The group started singing Christian songs, and it wasn't long until a large crowd of around eighty gathered to listen.

On April 10 and 11 they moved all the items from the old shop in town to the new shop at Bhusaldanda. Otho and Carl worked together to organize their tools and other items in their brand new work space.

Ten days later Otho and Earl went out to Bhusaldanda to the Elfgaards' for breakfast. Eleven coolies who were workers on the building site went along with them back to Tansen to carry the Timothys' organ and refrigerator to the hospital. Next, the coolies carried Otho's and Earl's belongings out to Bhusaldanda.

The two Pax men settled into one end of the first story of the Godown with a thin partition wall separating their room from the shop. They liked the convenience of once again living so close to where they worked. Otho installed shelves for their clothes and hung pictures on the walls. He took the boards from the crate that the Elfgaards' refrigerator had been packed in and made a wardrobe for his and Earl's

110

clothes. He also fixed up a board on the head end of his bed so he could sit up in bed and read. Earl fixed up one for his bed, too, and a board to use as a lap desk.

Otho wrote to his parents, *"Well, I have moved again, but this time only a mile. Earl and I fixed the one end of the workshop up, so we moved into it yesterday. Now we are here where our work is, and it is also a lot cooler here in our room than it was in the attic of the present hospital."*

Three months later, while Earl was in Kathmandu for the rainy season, Otho swept and washed the floor of a little room on the second story of the Godown and moved his and Earl's belongings into it. He would stay there until they could build a more permanent partition between their room on the first floor and the shop area next to it. Otho wrote in his diary that night, *"This is a much nicer room, the best I had since I came to Tansen."*

The Elfgaards moved into their new house at Bushaldanda on July 11.

In November the masons began work on the Friederickses' house. The family moved from town to the upstairs of the Godown the first part of December until their new house at Bhusaldanda was ready

Nepali workers carry the Friederickses' piano from Tansen to Bhusaldanda.

for them. When they moved the Friederickses' piano out to the land, it took three and a half hours of determination and the strength of twelve workers to carry it from Tansen to Bhusaldanda. The workers were proud of themselves after learning it had taken thirty men to carry it from Butwal to Tansen.

Also in November, the carpenters installed the permanent wall between Otho and Earl's room and the shop, installing a door between the two and a door from their room to the outside. They built wooden sills, whitewashed the walls, and laid floor bricks.

On Thanksgiving Day, November 28, one year after they arrived in Tansen, Otho and Earl moved back into their finished room. During the next several days, they installed shelves, brought a table into the room, and hung mottoes and pictures on the walls. Otho and Carna made a trip to the bazaar and bought cloth for curtains. The carpenters built a washstand for them and Otho sawed a hole in the top to set a basin in and placed a bucket underneath where they could pour the water. He also added a door with a lock to one of the shelves so he could keep money and other valuables in it.

Otho fixed up a rope on two rollers with one end attached to their door going into the shop and a weight on the other end to pull the door shut automatically when they went through it. This helped to keep the dust and dirt from the shop out of their room. He enjoyed living at Bhusaldanda and lived in the Godown for the rest of his time in Tansen.

CHAPTER 16

"Lord, Glorify Your Name"

Tansen, Nepal; March–November 1957

In March 1957 two young Christian men, Surendra and Sodemba, came from India to teach in Tansen. A month later two young women—Maner Martha Ria, a Nepali, and Dorcas David, an Indian—joined them. All four were part of the UMN Young Adult Literacy Program which taught Nepali adults how to read and told them about Jesus. They all spoke English fluently. Otho, Earl, Surendra, and Sodemba enjoyed doing activities together.

The work on the hospital buildings and the relationships with the Nepali people were going well. The missionaries felt good about the progress they were making in both humanitarian and spiritual aid to the people of Tansen.

But then amid the enthusiasm and progress came a damper: a visit from a Kathmandu government official one day in May. That afternoon the governor of Tansen called Carl Friedericks for a hearing where he told Carl that the adult literacy program must stop until they received written permission from Kathmandu. The governor also told him they could not preach their religion in Nepal and had

Otho with his two friends from India, Surendra and Sodemba

shown him an old law indicating punishment by jail for anyone who converted to another religion or who converted someone else. To add yet another grim twist, elections were coming soon. The foreigners knew this could mean they would no longer be welcome in Nepal, depending on who was elected.

Otho began to experience the difficulties and uncertainties of being a missionary as well as the joys and excitement. He told his parents in a letter: *"I often heard returned missionaries talking and a lot of them had stories to tell along the same lines, but I remember the words of one who said, 'Yes, the missionaries have a lot of wonderful experiences and stories to tell when they return to their own people, but,' he said, 'remember this: there is a difference in being a returned missionary and being a missionary on the field.' I find a lot of truth in that...."*

The saddened missionaries weren't the only ones who heard the news. The Nepalis also soon knew about the hearing and the law that prohibited them from preaching about Jesus. But it didn't seem to faze them. One of them said, "It's okay if they put us in jail. We can tell the people in jail about Jesus." This perspective from the Nepalis surprised them, but it was also a great encouragement.

Otho continued his letter to his parents, asking for their prayers and expressing his heart: *"Can we glory in tribulation or persecution? I say we can! 'Know ye not that your labor is not in vain in the Lord.' God has revealed to me that I cannot glory in myself or in the things that I do, but only in Him and His Cross. I have been asking God to glorify His Name here in Nepal. Now I can see Him doing it, and I believe that He will continue to, if we remain faithful to Him and walk in His path and give Him the glory."*

Sodemba and Surendra left to go home to India since they weren't allowed to teach. The elections came and went, and the missionaries were permitted to stay and continue building. As Otho had said, the Lord continued to glorify His Name in Nepal.

They saw the Lord glorify His Name in Tansen again six months later after a long fight to bring running water to Bhusaldanda for the hospital and the other buildings

In mid–April 1957, the Governor and several members of the council had come out to Bhusaldanda to look around after they had asked permission to tap into the town's main water line to pipe water to the new buildings. Although the council had approved it, some Nepalis were against Bhusaldanda getting water. For a long time, they were unsure if it would happen.

But in November the Nepali government gave its approval for them to get water from the town water line that ran along the edge of the hospital property. A Nepali plumber from Tansen, Ram Khrishna, and his workers started fitting the water pipes on Friday morning, November 8. Otho and Carl stood and watched, grateful they were finally getting water — a huge step forward for their building project.

The Nepali police force came and surrounded the hole to protect the men working on the pipes and the missionaries watching. Half an hour after the hole was drilled, a mob arrived, shouting angrily and

An exciting day — water comes to Bhusaldanda!

doing their best to push past the police to stop the work. Enraged, several of the missionaries' Nepali friends shouted and pushed back. By that time they were arguing more about politics than they were water. Otho and the other missionaries were grateful no real fights broke out and that the arguing didn't evolve beyond shouting and shoving.

Twice the plumbers were lacking something they needed. They were items Otho had in the shop, so both times he volunteered to retrieve them. Trusting the Lord for his safety, he felt no fear as he walked through the angry crowd to the shop and back again.

At three thirty that afternoon, the pipe was hooked up and water ran from the spigot. The missionaries grinned at each other in joy and gratitude. Their persistent effort to bring water to Bhusaldanda had finally succeeded.

The police left and the mob disbanded, leaving Bhusaldanda once more with peace — and running water.

CHAPTER 17

"TV Men" and a Journey

Tansen and Kathmandu, Nepal; June 1957

During the summer of 1957, the American Medical Association filmed a documentary titled *MD International*, featuring American doctors serving in Korea, Hong Kong, Burma, Sarawak, India, Lebanon, Ethiopia—and even a doctor named Carl Friedericks serving in Tansen, Nepal. It aired on television stations across the United States on Thursday, January 23, 1958, and today can be viewed online at: collections.nlm.nih.gov/catalog/nlm:nlmuid-8800933A-vid

On Wednesday, June 12, Earl headed down to Bhairawa to meet the "TV men," as Otho referred to them in his diary, who were coming from Kathmandu. Rudy Friesen, an MCC worker stationed in Kathmandu, had come along with them. They all arrived in Tansen on Friday.

The men filming the documentary—David Lowe (a producer and director from New York) and Lou Hazam (a writer from Silver Spring, Maryland)—focused on Dr. Friedericks' medical work in Tansen and the outlying areas. Because it didn't involve him, Otho went about his work as usual over the next number of days while the filming was taking place.

Carl (in white shirt and pants) talks to one of the "TV men" as they were getting ready to leave Tansen for Kathmandu accompanied by Earl (center), Otho, and Rudy.

A week later Otho, Earl, and Rudy packed their suitcases to join the TV men on their journey back to Kathmandu. While there, Otho and Earl would visit the Kathmandu missionaries and acquire visas that would allow them to travel monthly to Gorakhpur, India, for supplies and money. Gorakhpur is located one–hundred miles south of Tansen and was the nearest large city where they could buy food and hardware not available in Tansen. They could also withdraw cash for the mission and the missionaries since Tansen had no banks. After getting their visas in Kathmandu, Otho and Earl would travel to Gorakhpur before returning home to Tansen.

They left Tansen on Wednesday afternoon, June 19. Nine coolies carried the luggage and camera equipment. They trekked to the top of the first mountain and stopped for the night. Otho bedded down on the porch of the Nepali home where they were staying, but sleep wouldn't come until after one o'clock. An hour and a half later, a thunderstorm awakened him with rain pouring down on him through the grass roof over his bed. He moved inside. It was a short night. Up at five thirty, they were on the trail by six.

When they got to an old bridge, they stopped to wait for the coolies. The TV men wanted to film them crossing the river by bridge and then wading the river further down the trail.

After that Rudy and Otho left the rest to hike ahead to Butwal where they rented a Dodge Power Wagon to take them to Bhairawa. *"The worst ride I ever had,"* Otho noted in his diary. By the time they got to the airport, they'd missed the only plane leaving for Kathmandu that day. As they were standing on the porch of a building at the airport, a bad dust storm blew in. They stood back in a corner and covered their faces until it was over.

After the rest of the group arrived, they had supper and enjoyed watermelon, which Otho hadn't eaten for two years. They slept on the porch that night.

They flew to Pokhara the next day and then on to Kathmandu. They spent the week there interacting with the missionaries, helping to fix items in the hospital and assisting the TV men as they filmed

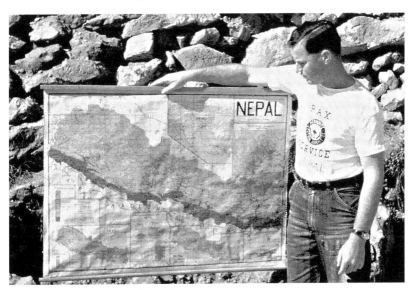

Otho with his new map of Nepal

The Swedish Mission in Gorakhpur, India, where Otho and Earl slept on the veranda because it was so hot

footage of Kathmandu and of Dr. Bethel Fleming at Shanta Bhawan, the former palace turned hospital. One day they went to the Indian Embassy Office and filled out forms for their visas to travel to India. Otho, Earl, and Rudy also tried to go shopping, but there was a strike. They did find one shop open where Otho bought a nice large map of Nepal—a visual he would use often after he returned home when he gave talks about Nepal. The map now hangs on the wall of his office.

Rudy drove Otho and Earl to the airport the morning of Friday, June 28, to fly to Bhairawa where they boarded a bus to Nautanwa, India. From there they traveled by train to Gorakhpur, India, and arrived that evening. A rickshaw (a three–wheeled bicycle) took them to the Swedish Mission where they would stay, but no one was there. The chowkidar let them in. It was stifling hot from being closed up. Otho boiled water to have potable water to drink, took a bath, and went to bed. There were no sheets, so they did without.

They shopped the following day for the food and hardware they had come for and packed it for the journey home. They slept on the veranda that night where it was cooler.

Leaving early the next morning, they took the train to Nautanwa and hopped on a bus, stopping at Bhairawa for customs. The police came on board to check all the passengers' passports and luggage. A commotion began, and Otho and Earl watched as the police led two men outside. They tied the men's hands to a post and beat them with a club, trying to force them to talk. Most of the other passengers got off and watched, but Otho and Earl stayed in their seats. They couldn't understand what was happening. Someone retrieved the men's suitcase and took it outside. The police opened it and took out a large dagger laying on top of the other contents.

Then they came on the bus and questioned Otho and Earl. "Do you know these two men? Are you traveling with them?"

"No," Otho and Earl told them. "We've never seen them before."

"Well, we suspect they've been following you," the police informed them.

After about an hour, the bus left Bhairawa. The two men were still tied to the post, and the police had possession of the dagger. Otho and Earl never learned what happened to the men or if they had truly been

After spending the night at a home in this little village of Butwal, Otho and Earl follow this trail through the town and gorge ahead to Tansen.

following them. They were grateful nothing worse than an hour's delay had taken place and thanked God for His protection.

The bus arrived in Butwal at four o'clock that afternoon, and by five they were on the trail. After hiking an hour, they crossed the river and found a Nepali home to stay in for the night. The rice, dal, eggs, and tea their hostess served them tasted especially good to them that evening. Their host gave them blankets and pillows, and they fell asleep on the veranda.

Up at four thirty the next morning, they hit the trail early and arrived in Tansen just before lunch. It had been quite a journey. After lunch and a bath, Otho crawled into bed and slept half the afternoon.

"Glad to be back home again," Otho wrote in his diary that night.

CHAPTER 18

A Costly Drink of Water

Tansen, Nepal and Gorakhpur, India; July–August 1957

Otho made his second trip to Gorakhpur for supplies a few weeks later. He and Earl awoke July 18 to a wet and rainy day. It wasn't the most pleasant for hiking, but they left Tansen by eight o'clock, regardless. It had already been raining for several days, and the trails were muddy and the river high. Not long after they started out, they had to stop for thirty minutes until the downpour slowed. They waded through water above their knees at seven different places on the trail, soaking their pants. The current was so strong it almost swept them off their feet.

When they got to Dhoban, the river was too high to cross, forcing them to take the route over another mountain to Butwal. That mountain turned out to be steep and rocky—the worst one Otho had ever crossed. They stayed at the Army Rest House overnight. It rained hard while they slept, but they awoke to a beautiful clear day.

Otho and Earl went to the bus station at eight and finally left on a bus three hours later. They reached Nautanwa, India, at two o'clock and took a pony cart to the railway station. There they caught a train and arrived in Gorakhpur at six thirty. A supper of fish and chips at the station tasted wonderful to the two travel–weary men. They hired a rickshaw to transport them to the Swedish Mission, which they discovered was full with other guests, so they booked a room at the hotel. Since it only had one bed, Otho slept on the floor.

Saturday was a hot day. They shopped for supplies in the forenoon and took shelter from the heat in the hotel in the afternoon. Earl left for Kathmandu by train that evening with plans to stay there for several weeks that summer.

The church service Otho attended the next morning was in Hindi. He enjoyed taking pictures that afternoon, capturing one of a monkey on a roof that had been making a lot of noise. After supper at the hotel, he sat at the table and talked with the people who ran it, learning they were from Portugal.

Otho spent the next two days continuing to buy supplies. He also went to the bank to withdraw cash for the mission and several of the missionaries. They were hot days, but he pushed through them so he could leave for Tansen on Wednesday morning.

He awoke during his last night in the hotel feeling parched and dehydrated from the heat. The only water available was from the hand pump in his room. Otho knew it was a risk to drink the unboiled water, but he was so thirsty, he drank it anyway.

He left by train at seven the following morning with four big boxes of supplies to take back with him to Tansen. When he arrived in Nautanwa mid–morning, he hired four coolies to carry the boxes over to their agent, Kadar North. There, he picked up a package from his brother Irvin and family and one for Carl that contained a motor part.

Otho met the two o'clock train bringing Dr. Helen Ramsey and Shamka Marvi (the Friederickses' servant) who were on their way to Tansen and planned to travel there with him. A truck took them to the Army Rest House in Butwal where they stayed for the night

The next day was rainy, but Otho was up early to arrange for coolies to carry the supplies they had bought back to Tansen. They left

Butwal by noon and got to the river at two. It was so deep that coolies were there to carry them across. But Otho had a dilemma. All the cash he had withdrawn was in his pants pockets. He didn't want it to get wet, but neither did he want the coolies to know he had it. He discussed it quietly with Dr. Ramsey.

"You have underwear on, don't you?" she asked him.

"Of course," Otho replied.

"Well, why don't you take off your pants and carry them?" she suggested. So, he did. He held his pants above his head as they crossed the river, riding on the shoulders of the coolies.

The water was up to the coolies' necks. They linked arms, with the lead coolie carrying a large rock to keep the current from carrying them away. They walked diagonally across the river against the current. Halfway across, they changed direction and walked diagonally with the current, arriving safely on the other side.

"Some experience!" he wrote later in his diary.

Otho and the two ladies walked on from there and stayed in Marrack that night, enjoying rice and dal with hot dogs that Dr. Ramsey had brought along with her from Landour, India. *"Boy, were they*

Otho enjoys a short break and some refreshment while hiking the mountainous trails from Gorkapur, India, back to Tansen in the heat.

125

good," Otho commented in his diary. They were the first hot dogs he'd eaten in a long time.

The next day, Friday, July 26, it rained just enough to keep the air cool, making the hike on the mountainous trail pleasant. They met the horse boy with the mission horse partway down the mountain. After reaching the bottom, the women took turns riding the horse on the two–hour trek across the valley. They arrived at the hospital in Tansen mid afternoon.

Toward evening, Otho went to meet the coolies carrying their boxes of supplies and followed them up to the hospital. He put his belongings in a pack to take out to Bhusaldanda. The chowkidar met him on the way to Bhusaldanda and carried his pack the rest of the way.

After supper and washing up, he read letters from his Mother and sister Ethel that had arrived while he was away. He also opened the package from his brother Irvin and family. What a treat! It contained a pound of Jelly Beans spilled all over the box, thirteen candy bars, five packages of Lifesavers, one box of tooth powder (even though the customs paper said there were two), twenty–three packages of chewing gum, one box of throat discs, one can of Spam, one pound of packaged cookies broken into pieces from traveling halfway around the world, and two packages of crackers similarly disassembled.

Some of the candy was chocolate — moldy chocolate, it turned out, from spending nine months en route from Maryland to Tansen. Otho was about to to throw it away, but Carna stopped him.

"No, you're not!" she told him and reached for it.

Otho gladly gave it to her. She cut off the mold, ate the candy, and declared, "This is the best chocolate I've had since I left Sweden!"

After his initial sampling of the goodies that evening, eating the rest of the treats would have to wait. By the next day Otho was feeling sick. Ragnar took Otho's turn preaching on Sunday because he wasn't feeling any better. Otho struggled through the next two weeks as he tried to get work done but continued to have diarrhea and to not feel well. One night, ten days after he'd gotten back, he was up every hour.

Otho enjoyed living in the Godown (two-story building on the right)
except when he became ill during the night and realized he was alone at
Bhusaldanda except for the Elfgaards in their own house (two-story building
on the left) and no way to communicate with them.

He finally walked the mile into Tansen to the hospital. Carna gave him
some brown pills for diarrhea which seemed to help. But during the
following night, he woke with swollen hands and feet. This scared him.
He was in the Godown alone with only the Elfgaards at Bhusaldanda
with him. But they were in their own house a little distance away, and
he had no means of contacting them. He got up and unlocked the door
so someone could enter if he continued to get worse during the night.

The next morning he was unable to walk to the Elfgaards' for
breakfast because his feet were so swollen. Knowing something had
to be wrong when Otho didn't show up, they came to check on him.
Carna thought the swelling was an allergic reaction to the brown pills
she'd given him and told him to stop taking them. She and Ragnar
wanted him to go to the hospital, but Otho didn't think he could make
it with his swollen feet. So Dr. Pedley, a new doctor who had arrived a
couple weeks before, came out to see him. He agreed with Carna that
Otho was having a reaction to the medicine.

After stopping the pills, the swelling went down, but the diarrhea
got worse. Eventually the illness ran its course. Otho finally recov-

ered, twenty pounds lighter. He had arrived in Tansen weighing 180 pounds from eating the fresh homemade bread and apple butter he had enjoyed so much while working in Germany. On his five-foot-ten inches frame, those extra pounds caused the Nepali workers to refer to him affectionately as "fat boy." After Otho's illness, they could no longer call him that.

At first no one knew what had made him so sick. Then Otho recalled drinking the unboiled water from the pump in his hotel room in Gorakhpur. He was grateful the Lord had protected him from worse. God still had work for him to do!

CHAPTER 19

One Big Happy Family

Tansen, Nepal; 1957

As Otho experienced during his illness, the missionaries operated as one big family. They not only worked together and looked out for each other, they played together, too.

Many evenings found them gathered to play games or to talk over coffee. Often two or three of them would get into deep discussions about the church in Nepal or India, the differences between Nepal and their home countries, and any other world problem they could try to solve. Sometimes they would fire up the generator to view slides or listen to their vinyl records. Some evenings they would sing, both in English and in Nepali, and would often include their Nepali friends.

The missionaries also took time off to celebrate each other's birthdays and the holidays of their various countries of origin. They enjoyed picnics, hikes, watching a play or sports in Tansen, and shopping in the bazaar.

Carl described the interaction between the missionaries in Odd Hoftun's book, *Power for Nepal*: *"Most of us found the differences [between us] interesting and even stimulating. This great diversity helped*

us to better understand the wideness of God's Kingdom and the gifts He has given his people. He sent the right people at the right time. It was a group of outstanding people, living well together, and each contributing to the developing philosophy. In this pioneering and often primitive situation, people had to be adaptable, ready to share and cooperate, be patient and trusting of others, and have a good sense of

Jimmy Friedericks enjoys a ride in Otho's knapsack.

humor. We worked together, we planned together, we prayed together, and we played together"* (Peter Svalheim, *Power for Nepal*, Martin Chautari 2015).

The sense of humor that eased the difficulties in their work and smoothed over their differences showed up in various ways, including teasing and practical jokes. On one occasion when they were all together, Carna told Otho to get down on his hands and knees and put his head down on the floor. He dutifully followed her instructions, unsuspecting of his kind, gentle friend.

"Repeat after me," she told him. "I know my heart."

"I know my heart," he repeated.

"I know my mind."

Otho and Earl picnic with the Friedericks family outside Tansen.

"I know my mind."

"I know that I stick up behind."

"CARNA!" Otho yelled as the room erupted in laughter. He'd been had, but it was all in good fun.

On the first Sunday in January, Otho, Earl, and the Friedericks family climbed the big hill behind Tansen for a picnic lunch. From that hill they had a good view of the town and could see the "snowies," as they called the snow-capped mountains of the Himalayas. But on this outing the clouds hid them from sight. On the return trip Otho carried a tired little Jimmy Friedericks on his back in Earl's knapsack.

On another Sunday in late January, Otho, Earl, Marjory, and Ingeborg set out for a picnic lunch, walking about three or four miles west of Tansen. It was a lovely walk, crossing several pretty fields. They ate beside a stream with steep hills on either side.

Otho enjoyed relating to the children of his fellow missionaries and would sometimes read to the younger ones. One evening after supper, little Lasse was crying. Otho picked him up and held him in a rocking chair until he fell asleep. Then Lillan crawled up on his lap with a book, and he read it to her. She spoke three languages (Swedish, Nepali, and Hindi) and understood English. Otho would speak to her in English and she would reply in Nepali, each understanding enough of the other's spoken language that they communicated just fine.

One day Carl, Betty, Richie, and Anne went on a picnic and left little Chucky Friedericks behind with Otho. Otho and Chucky enjoyed eating lunch together—just the two of them. It brought back fond memories for Otho of the times he and little Lynn ate lunch together when Lula was away and the girls were in school.

For Richie Friederick's tenth birthday on January 9, Otho made him a little spool tractor. And for Lillan Elfgaard's fourth birthday on May 1, Otho made her a chair just her size.

Otho and the other missionaries started building a tennis court out on the land toward the

Lillan Elfgaard tries out the chair Otho made for her fourth birthday.

end of January. It would provide them with many hours of fun and exercise — both in playing tennis and chasing the ball when it went down the hill. Sometimes it took twenty minutes to find the ball and climb back up to the court. By then they had all the exercise they wanted and had lost interest in running around on a tennis court. When the Elfgaards' dog, Kalo, started bounding down the hill to fetch the ball for them, everyone was delighted, including Kalo. They could keep playing with another ball and Kalo got his fun and exercise, too. He would lie off to the side of the tennis court while they played, just waiting for a ball to bounce over the side of the hill.

A nice day in late February found Otho, Earl, and the Friedericks family hiking outside of Tansen past the land for a picnic lunch. Afterward the rest went back to town while Otho, Carl, and Richie walked

Ragnar and Earl play tennis with Mr. Oliver, executive director of UMN, while the Elfgaards' dog, Kalo, eagerly waits to fetch any stray balls.

another four miles looking for a place to camp. It was Otho's first camping trip. They set up a tent and then looked around for wood for a campfire. They discovered the Nepalis had already gathered most of it for their use, but found plenty of smaller sticks. It was enough to build a fire to cook their meal of fish, cream of chicken soup, baked beans with pork, corn, cheese, and coffee.

Otho woke often during his first night of camping but felt surprisingly refreshed in the morning. They started another fire to make coffee and ate puffed rice, hard boiled eggs, and cinnamon buns for breakfast. As they made their way down the trail toward home, they saw a prickly pear plant, much like cactus, and Carl cut off a pear for them to eat. Otho had never eaten one before but found it delicious.

After they got back that evening, Otho, the Friedericks family, Earl, Marjory, Ingeborg, and Emma, went to the Johns' house where they ate an Indian meal of rice and dal, potatoes, onions, chicken, sweet rice, a cabbage salad, and Nepali tea. They sat on the floor and ate with their hands, Indian and Nepali style. Although Otho had watched the Nepalis do this many times, it was the first he tried it. Somehow he thought the food tasted better this way!

Personal matters had to be taken care of, too. In the absence of dentists and barbers, in particular, they helped each other.

March 18 found Earl in bed with a sinus infection, so Otho went out to the land to take his place overseeing the workers. All day Otho's upper left wisdom tooth hurt him so badly he didn't do much but sit and watch the workers.

That evening Ragnar, who had limited training in dentistry

Carl and Richie hike ahead of Otho to find a place to camp.

and often pulled teeth for the Nepali people, offered to pull it for him. Otho sat in a chair in the hospital garden, and Carl gave him a shot of Novocain. Ragnar went to work, but it wasn't an easy extraction. The tooth broke off with the roots still intact. He worked hard to get those roots out and was ready to give up several times, but then would say, "I'll try again." Carl said he could remove them surgically if needed. Finally, all the roots were out. Otho was relieved and wrote in his diary that night, *"I'm glad he got it all out, because I didn't want to go through that again!"* Carl gave Otho pain pills and one of the ward boys gave him a shot of penicillin. He went to bed early but didn't sleep well because of the bleeding. He stayed in bed for most of the next day.

Another of Otho's teeth caused him a lot of pain a couple months later. Since Ragnar wasn't there, Carl pulled it for him. Otho recorded in his diary that it was seven–eighths inch long with the roots a half inch long.

Later that year Otho tried his hand at dentistry. Rudy Friesen, one of the MCC workers stationed in Kathmandu, was visiting and needed a tooth pulled. Otho assisted while Ragnar did the honors.

In August Otho added "barber" to his resume of tasks accomplished while in Nepal. He and Ragnar both needed haircuts, so they cut each other's hair. It was a first for both, although Otho had once tried cutting his younger brother Luke's hair at home. Otho wrote in his diary afterward, *"We don't look too half bad, and no one said anything about it."* They were both satisfied enough that two months later they gave each other haircuts again.

They observed the Swedish tradition of greeting spring on May 1, by rising early and going to the top of the hill for coffee. It was also Lillan Elfgaard's birthday, so they gathered again later in the day for coffee and birthday cake.

A couple weeks later, the workers brought a dead animal that looked like a porcupine. They pulled out its pins, cut off its head, held it over the fire, then scraped it with sticks and a piece of tin. They cut it open and gutted it, then cut up the meat into pieces and divided it between

Carna holds Lasse as she watches the workers butcher the mystery animal.

them. They even divided the insides. Otho wanted to try it, so Carna bought one Rupee's worth—a half pound—and prepared it for supper. Ragnar commented several times how good the meat was. He asked Carna what it was, but she avoided his question, partly because she didn't know. He kept asking. Finally she told him she wasn't sure, but it looked like a rat. That was it—he wouldn't eat another bite! Otho rather liked it, though, and noted in his diary, *"I didn't think it was too bad."*

The missionaries celebrated Otho's and Earl's birthdays on May 25, inviting the whole hospital staff to a birthday party for them. Earl's birthday was the next day, and Otho gave him a safety razor. On the morning of Otho's 24th birthday, June 5, the Elfgaards woke him by singing to him and serving him cake and coffee in bed. They also gave him a wide woolen belt to go with his Nepali outfit.

In September Mary Cundy from England joined the missionary family. She would be taking over Ragnar's work when the Elfgaards left for furlough.

Otho "visited" Germany most of the afternoon on Sunday, October 27, by looking at his slides from Germany. It brought back many good memories of his time there. It wasn't until Carl mentioned at supper that the Suez trouble took place one year before that it occurred to Otho it was exactly a year to the day that he and Earl had left Germany to come to Nepal.

He noted in his diary on November 12 that it was *"1 year ago today I landed in Nepal for the first time, at Kathmandu."*

Thanksgiving Day came on November 29. They ate Thanksgiving dinner with the Friedrickses, then held a short service in the meeting room and a party for those working at the hospital.

Otho had thoroughly enjoyed his first full year in Tansen. Never in his wildest dreams would he have guessed a remote town in Nepal would become home to him. But here he was, halfway around the world from his big family in Maryland, enjoying his new big family in Nepal.

CHAPTER 20

Christmas in India

Dhamtari, India; December 1957

When Otho had traveled with the Paul Miller family by ship on his way to Nepal, they had discussed the possibility of Otho spending some of his vacation time with them in India. Some time later, he received a letter from the Millers inviting him to come for Christmas.

Otho left Tansen on Monday, December 16, 1957, after sending a coolie off with his baggage a couple hours earlier to get a head start. He spent the night at the mission in Butwal and left by bus the next morning for Nautanwa, India. Once there, he cleaned up a little and shaved before leaving on the ten o'clock train that night.

Settled on the train packed full of passengers and exhausted from two long days of travel, Otho struggled to stay awake so he could keep an eye on his belongings. He sat on some of his things and had the rest close by to protect as best he could. When he couldn't keep his eyes open any longer, he prayed silently, "Lord, I can't stay awake and watch this stuff, but I know You're awake all the time, so I commit it all to You," and drifted off to sleep. When he awoke later, refreshed, all of his belongings were still there.

Arriving at the Allahabad station at nine o'clock the next morning, Otho rode by rickshaw to the Allahabad Junction Station and caught the Bombay Mail train to Katni. He again rode the rails through the night, arriving in Raipur at noon on Thursday. From there he took a bus to Dhamtari and arrived mid-afternoon. A rickshaw took him to the hospital where several missionaries gave him a ride to the Miller's home, eighteen miles outside of Dhamtari.

Otho enjoyed a mostly relaxed two-week vacation there, catching up with the Millers and other missionaries and seeing their work in India. They included him in their Christmas gift exchange. Paul had his name and gave Otho a beautiful tiger carved from a buffalo horn. Otho had drawn Jacob Flisher's name and presented him with a kukri (a Nepali knife).

On Christmas Day the Millers and Otho went to an outlying village for a church service and were invited to two different homes for lunch. Wanting to honor both families, they went to both. As they were almost ready to leave the second house, a woman came in the back door and asked them to come to her house to get something to eat. The missionaries agreed and went. Just as they were about to leave there, yet another Indian man came and invited them for a meal. Not wanting to offend him, they went there, too. The stuffed crew piled into the car and headed home. But soon after they arrived, an elderly lady invited them to her house where they managed to eat their fifth

Otho spends Christmas with the the Miller family at their house in India.

The Millers and Otho attend an Indian wedding.

Indian meal. Otho was grateful the Millers had warned him before going to the first home not to eat too much, knowing the likelihood they would be invited to several places for meals that day.

Two days later they attended an Indian wedding. The groom invited them to his house to ride along to pick up the bride and her family to take them to the church.

On the way back to the Millers', they traveled through the jungle and saw many beautiful peacocks. One of the men shot one, and they enjoyed it for supper the next day.

Otho showed slides of Nepal in the Dhandari Church on the last Sunday of 1957. He wrote in his diary, *"The first time I showed them in a church."* But it wouldn't be the last. He would share them many more times in churches in the years to come.

On the first day of 1958, Otho, Paul Miller, and Paul's son James awoke at six to go hunting in the Mangal–Tarai jungle. Two other missionaries, Jacob Flisher and Alvin Hostetler, accompanied them.

Otho and Alvin were sitting together on the ground just outside the jungle when a cheetah sprang out of the jungle heading straight towards them. Stopping just fifty feet away, the big cat looked straight at the two men. Alvin quickly raised his shotgun and pulled the trigger. The cheetah dropped to the ground. He shot it a second time to

Indians carry the dead cheetah Alvin Hostetler shot.

make sure it was dead. Otho didn't have time to be frightened at the time but felt rattled later thinking about what could have happened.

He left the Millers' house on January 3 and arrived in Gorakhpur by train two days later. It was early Sunday morning. He enjoyed a big breakfast in the station before traveling by rickshaw to the Swedish Mission where he met Odd and Tullis Hoftun from Norway for the first time. They were on their way to Kathmandu but would soon arrive in Tansen to join the work there.

While waiting for a train, Otho bought several oranges and started eating one. A beggar came up to him and asked for money. Otho had heard that many of the beggars were placed in areas like train stations by enterprising individuals who took most of the money they collected, leaving the beggars with only a small percentage. Knowing this, Otho gave him some of his orange rather than money. Soon more beggars came, and Otho gave away all his oranges, piece by piece. They all went away happy, and Otho felt satisfied that he'd been able to give them something to eat instead of padding someone else's pockets.

While in Gorakhpur, Otho had bought supplies and withdrawn cash and packed them in a suitcase. The missionary who took him to the train station helped him carry his luggage onto the train. Otho put the suitcase holding the money in the overhead compartment across the aisle from his seat so he could keep it in sight. As the missionary was leaving, he pointed to the suitcase and told Otho, "Keep an eye on that bag."

Otho nodded and glanced around nervously, wondering who else may have heard him. Again he committed his luggage to the Lord and was relieved and grateful when he arrived in Tansen and the money was safely in the right hands.

It was January 9, and he was glad to be home and ready to get back to his normal life and work in Tansen. But while he was away, plans had been made for him to take another journey.

CHAPTER 21

Six Days By Foot To Amppipal

Amppipal, Nepal; January 1958

When Otho got back from his trip to India, he learned that he and Earl were scheduled to go to the mission in Amppipal to help finish a house for UMN missionary Jonathan Lindell and his family. Otho had just one full day in Tansen before leaving again.

Amppipal is about 90 miles east of Tansen and halfway between Pokhara and Kathmandu. The trip would take six days by foot through the rugged mountains. They would travel without coolies this time, each carrying their own forty pound rucksack. Although the extra weight would cause them to stop more often to rest, they believed they could travel faster on their own than hiring coolies to carry their luggage.

Sporting the stubble of a beard from not being able to shave on his trip home from India, Otho decided to let it grow. Six days on the trail would provide no opportunities to shave, anyway—just baths in the river when they could.

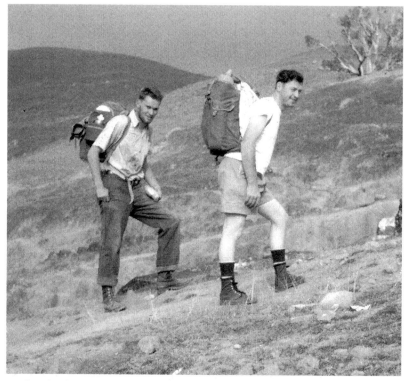

Earl and Otho leave Tansen to hike six days to Amppipal in the Gorkha District.

Otho and Earl left Tansen the morning of January 11, getting to the river by noon and then to a leprosy colony by two thirty. Otho had seen photos of lepers, but this was the first he observed in person how the disease eats away the flesh of its victims, including whole body parts such as hands, feet, and noses. It was heartbreaking to Otho to see women with small children and one even nursing her baby.

The two Pax men were quite a curiosity there, with many from the village coming out to the house where they were spending the night to get a good look at them. The spectators would sit awhile and then get up and leave. By six thirty the two men were so tired from their first day of walking with their heavy packs, they crawled into the sleeping bags they had borrowed from Carl and were soon asleep.

Twelve hours later, Otho and Earl awoke refreshed. To communicate to their hostess they wanted boiled water for coffee, they made the sound of water bubbling when it boils, and she understood. Fueled by a good night's rest and their morning coffee, they were back on the trail a half hour later for the second day of their journey. At noon they stopped for tea at a lady's home in the Andhi Khola valley where they had stayed before. Soon after they arrived, they discovered she was sick. She indicated she wanted pills. Earl gave her the only thing he had with him — Lifesavers. She was satisfied. After drinking their tea, Otho and Earl were on their way again. They stayed at a home in the valley that night and washed in the river.

On the morning of their third day of travel, they continued walking through the valley for three hours before starting to climb a mountain. The trail on the other side had steps the whole way down the mountain. It was an exhausting way to descend. They walked in the dry river bed for a while and crossed two more mountains before coming to the Pokhara Valley in the evening when it was dark. They were further south than they had thought they were. Asking someone for directions only sent them off on another wrong trail. After forty-five minutes, they came out on the airfield and realized they had walked in a huge circle. Finally they

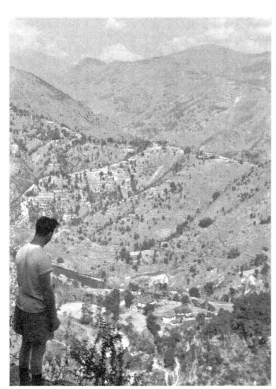

Otho enjoys the view before descending the mountain into the Andhi Khola valley.

Seeing leprosy and its effect on those infected with the awful disease was heartrending for Otho and Earl, but a harsh reality for many.

got on the trail leading into the bazaar. But again they made a wrong turn, going through the busiest section of town. Otho and Earl eventually arrived at the Pokhara Mission at eight o'clock. Exhausted, they ate supper and soon went to bed.

In the morning they enjoyed breakfast with three English missionary women. The two men accompanied the ladies to the other side of the airfield, about an hour walk from the hospital. There they met three other ladies who worked at the leprosarium in Pokhara. They showed the two men around and explained their work with the lepers. Otho admired their efforts and was glad to know those with this dreaded disease were receiving help.

Leaving Pokhara the next morning, Otho and Earl walked through the long valley and climbed a mountain. At the peak a thunderstorm came up. They continued hiking in the rain until they reached Deorali where they stopped at a house for tea. While they were drinking their tea, the rain poured even harder, so they decided to stay there for the night.

A good Nepali meal for breakfast early the following morning fueled them for the day. Then they were on the trail, crossing the river Sisaghat in a dugout boat four hours later. They climbed the mountain to Kunchha and descended to a valley to Tarkughat. There they spent the night in a filthy room. Otho thought it looked like a chicken house and Earl called it a pig pen.

They crossed the river at Chepe Ghat in the morning and started to climb again until finally arriving at Amppipal at one thirty. The missionaries welcomed them and showed them around. The two fellows fixed up their beds in a storage room where they would sleep during their time in Amppipal.

For the next ten days, Otho and Earl helped with the Lindells' house. They built a stairway—a first for both—in one day. That night, Otho

The two Pax men enjoy social time with the Lindells and the other missionaries during their time in Amppipal.

Otho and Earl help complete a house for UMN missionary Jonathan Lindel and his family.

wrote in his diary, *"We were both surprised that we built it so fast and good. It looks right good for the first time, if we do have to say so ourselves."*

Another day they had the challenging job of laying down flooring using crooked boards in different thicknesses. They got it done after much sawing, planing, chopping, and blocking up of each board.

Otho and Earl thoroughly enjoyed the interaction with the missionaries in Amppipal, including two delightful picnics. One evening Earl played the trumpet, Ron (a missionary from England) played the trombone, and Otho sang. Before Otho went to bed the last work day in Amppipal, he observed in his diary, *"The house looks a little different now than what it did a week ago."* It was satisfying to have accomplished what they came to do.

The first day of their trip home was a rainy one, slowing them down and requiring them to seek shelter a couple times, once under a tree and another time in a shack. That night they stayed in a leaf shack—a simple structure with no walls, just a roof made of leaves.

The following day they crossed the river at Sisaghat on a ferry. They were surprised to meet Surendra along the trail and stopped to visit for a pleasant twenty–minute break. They slept in a hut that night in Bujapur.

The leprosarium in Pokhara was their first stop in the morning, where they ate breakfast. They met Odd and Tullis Hoftun, who were

Earl crosses a stream on their trek home to Tansen.

on their way to join the work in Tansen, at the airfield just as their plane was ready to leave. Then Otho and Earl continued their journey, but it soon began to rain. Otho bought an umbrella, and Earl covered his pack with a sheet of plastic so they could continue on in the rain for the three hours it took to climb to the top of the next mountain, Nuwakot. They ate lunch before descending in the afternoon. Belbari, a two-hour walk into the valley, was their stop for the night.

An early morning start on January 30 got them to the end of the valley by mid-morning and to the bridge crossing the river by four o'clock. Since they were making such good time, they continued on until they got home to Bhusaldanda at eight that evening. It had been a long tiring day of walking.

Betty prepared a hot meal for them before they took baths to sooth their aching muscles. Otho read his mail and caught up on news from home. After spending most of the month of January elsewhere, he was ready to get back into the normal routine of life and work in Tansen.

CHAPTER 22

1958 Brings Changes

Tansen, Nepal; February 1958

*C*hanges in Tansen were on the horizon. One had already taken place while Otho was in Amppipal: the first electricity in Tansen had been installed in several of the new houses at Bhusaldanda.

But even more significant for Otho were the changes in missionary personnel. On the day Otho and Earl arrived back in Tansen, Odd and Tullis Hoftun had also arrived. Odd was an electrical engineer from Norway. His role would be to manage the construction of the hospital buildings. He would prove to have a significant role in Nepal in the years to come. After completing the hospital in Tansen, he would move on to work at harnessing the power of Nepal's rivers to give its people

Tullis and Odd Hoftun

hydro–power. His biography, *Power for Nepal* by Peter Svalheim and published in 2015, tells that fascinating story. While working with the Nepalis to build the Tansen hospital, he would come to realize they could accomplish much for Nepal with little cost by utilizing its natural resources and training the Nepalis to do the labor.

In addition to welcoming the Hoftuns that February, Otho also said some difficult goodbyes to fellow missionaries. Ragnar and Carna Elfgaard and their family were leaving February 4 for their home in Sweden, and wouldn't return until November 1959—after Otho had finished his term of service in Nepal and left for his home in Maryland. And at the end of the month, Earl would complete his term of Pax service and return to his home in Canada.

Ragnar turned over the financial books for the building fund to Otho the day after Otho returned from Amppipal. He now had the responsibility of paying the bills for the building project as well as the Nepali workers' salaries.

The Trail-side Diner staff: Khrishna, Betty Anne, Richard, Earl, Otho, and Carl

Otho takes a picture of Yogan and the Elfgaards before saying goodbye to the family he had come to love.

On February 1 the missionaries had a party to say goodbye to the Elfgaards and to welcome the Hoftuns and a Christian Nepali nurse and his wife from Raxaul.

Otho, Earl, Carl, and Betty Anne planned an additional farewell party for the Elfgaards. Otho and Earl got busy making signs and caps for their made-up "Trail-side Diner" and its "staff." Otho typed up four copies of the three songs they'd written for the evening: "Santa Lucia," "All You Ate'a" to the tune "Alouette," and "When the Swedes go Sailing Home" to the tune of "When the Saints Go Marching In." Carl was the prep cook named "Jake," Betty Anne a waitress named "Sweetie-Pie," Richard a bus boy called "Pete," Earl a waiter named "Lewy," Khrishna Bahadur an assistant cook called "Handsome," and Otho was "Hank" the chef.

Everyone had a great time. They finished the evening with a program of music and skits. At the end they sang Auld Lang Syne and prayed together.

The Elfgaards left the morning of February 4 from Bhusaldanda. They stopped at the Hospital for a while to say their goodbyes. Otho and Yogan walked along with them to the valley where Otho snapped pictures of the Elfgaards on the trail. After saying goodbye to this dear family that had become like his own, he stood and watched as they continued on down the trail with thirteen coolies carrying their belongings.

With only weeks left until Earl was to leave, the two Pax men packed several fun activities into their schedule. They wrote a song to the tune of, "I Am Just a Weary Pilgrim," and made signs of each phrase in the song. Staging scenes with the signs, they took pictures illustrating each phrase:

I am just a weary Pax man,
Plodding through this land of Nepal
Carrying packs and boiled water
Always eating rice and dal.
Oh yes there's Pax service in Nepal
Oh yes there's Pax service in Nepal
Oh what a grand experience
Was the Pax service in Nepal.

One day Otho, Earl, and the Friedericks family went up on Srinagar Danda (hill) for a picnic. Afterward Otho, Earl, Carl, and Richard carried their backpacks down on the other side and camped for the night. They cooked their own supper over the campfire and enjoyed soup, salmon, rolls, coffee, and brownies.

In the morning breakfast was a joint effort. Richard and Otho started the campfire and then Otho mixed up the pan-

Otho sports a beard after days on the trail.

154

Betty Anne walks with Annie, Richie, and Earl a little way down the trail as they leave Tansen with coolies carrying their luggage.

cake batter. Carl fried the eggs while Earl flipped the pancakes. It was a fun getaway for the men, and Richie especially enjoyed it. They got back to Bhusaldanda at ten o'clock in time for morning prayer with the workers.

Otho and Earl also made a softball bat out of pine wood that month. They took several staff boys up to Srinagar for a game of softball, the first ever played in Tansen. Otho's team lost 17–14.

Another day they set up Carl's photo enlargers and printed pictures for Earl to take along home. They also printed photos to send along with Earl to mail to Otho's parents. One picture Otho printed for them was of himself with a beard. Otho placed it on top of the stack of pictures and put them in an envelope.

He later heard his parents' side of the story when they received the pictures. Pop picked up their mail at the post office in Clear Spring and opened the envelope before he got home. When he walked into

Earl holds Roger as he says good-bye to Otho, the last the two friends will see each other for more than fifty years.

the kitchen at home, he showed his wife the picture of Otho with a beard. Covering Otho's eyes and forehead with his hand, Pop asked her who it was. She didn't know until Pop removed his hand. Then she recognized her son by his smiling eyes!

By that time Otho had become weary of his full beard, which made his face itchy. He got busy one afternoon cutting and shaving it off. It was quite the job. He determined to never grow out his beard again and to this day, never has.

On February 27 Otho and Earl rose early. It was the day of Earl's departure. Richie and Annie were traveling with Earl to India where they attended boarding school. Otho and Betty Anne walked with them down the trail to the valley. There, he and Earl said their goodbyes. They had thoroughly enjoyed traveling, working, and living together. Otho was sorry to see him leave, but Earl's work in Nepal was finished, while God still had work there for him to do.

CHAPTER 23

The Work Continues

When Otho got back to Buhusaldanda after saying good-bye to Earl, he jumped into his new role of filling some of Ragnar's responsibilities. His work would now focus on the building project rather than just tasks in the shop. He would serve as building supervisor — overseeing the project and the Nepali workers.

That afternoon Otho, Carl, and Odd looked around the building site to orient themselves for the work ahead. From that point on, many similar discussions would take place as they planned the next phases of the building process.

The first day that Otho paid the workers' salaries, he walked into Tansen to get the money from Master Ji, a Nepali that worked at the hospital. Otho carried the 2,079 rupees in a bag on his back out to the hospital. Curious about how much it weighed, he set the bag on the scales and watched the needle settle at fifty pounds. He paid the workers their salaries that afternoon.

Money began to run low in the building fund. Otho, Odd, and Carl discussed what to do. Afterward, they met with Dharma Ratna, the

Otho pays the coolies who carried wood for the builders.

head carpenter, and Kanooge, the head mason. Carl explained their building plans for the next couple months including the need to dismiss all the workers except for twelve until they had more funds. This meant Otho, Odd, and Carl would need to do more of the hands–on work to keep building. Later they dismissed all the workers except the carpenters for two weeks to give the carpenters a chance to catch up.

While the workers were fewer, the attendance at the Nepali church services increased almost double what it had been months before and included some of Marjory's patients at the hospital. One man, Attan, would sometimes give the message. Otho enjoyed watching him speak even though he couldn't understand everything he was saying in Nepali.

At one service Bhim Bahadur, one of the workers, came wearing a light jacket. Otho couldn't help but smile as he recognized the fabric from a pair of pajamas Earl had given him.

In April Odd made a trip to India and brought Munna Samuel Eklof, an Indian Swedish Baptist, back with him. Munna had been adopted by Miss Eklof, a Swedish missionary, when he was young. He spoke Hindi, Odu, Swedish, and English. His job would be working in the shop. The next morning after his arrival, he joined Otho, Odd, and Carl in their discussion about the building project.

One morning in April, Otho, Carl, Ieuan, Budri (who worked in the hospital), Bir Bahadur (one of the workers), and Munna went out to a Brahman village (Dharlumdara) to spray DDT, walking two hours to get there by evening. They stayed in the school house for the night.

Waking at five thirty the next morning, they walked half a mile down the hill to a nice spring to wash up before eating a little breakfast. Then they got to work spraying. Otho, Budri, and Munna sprayed the one–hundred or so buildings in the village. Most of them were dark and full of flies. In some of the houses, Otho had to feel his way up long stairways to the second floor.

Meanwhile, Carl examined some adults and children for smallpox, and Ieuan and Bir Bahadur gave four–hundred cholera shots.

They left a little after five that evening, arriving back at Buhusaldanda tired, hungry, and ready for baths and a big supper.

At the end of April the missionaries met and elected a building committee comprised of Odd, Carl, Marjory, and Otho. The committee's first meeting lasted four hours. At another meeting they decided

Matthew, Odd, John, and Munna at the building site

to build house number four with two apartments that would accommodate two single ladies in each.

They invited thirteen leading men of the town out to the land in early May to show them how they planned to build housing for families of hospital patients to stay in. They wanted their input on how the Nepalis would prefer various features, such as the kitchens and toilets.

That evening they held a committee meeting that lasted until ten thirty. Otho tried to relax afterward with a bath and crawled into bed after eleven. But sleep wouldn't come until two in the morning. Too many thoughts were circling around in his head about their plans.

Otho was thoroughly enjoying his work. As he looked ahead to the end of his Pax term, he recognized the benefits of continuity to the project if he would stay longer to help complete the buildings. He wrote a letter to Bob Miller at MCC, asking to extend his term another year. He would have to wait several weeks for a response.

In the meantime, his work continued. He divided his time between paying bills and salaries, overseeing the workers, making and repairing things, and doing whatever needed to be done. He enjoyed the variety of tasks. From one day to the next he might be explaining to the workers how to clear out a septic tank, figuring out how much to pay whom, helping the blacksmith cut and bend tin for a roof, sharpening

Otho checks in the workers before they begin work in the morning. Yogan stands behind him to interpret.

Carl discusses the model of the new hospital complex with Master Ji. The Godown sits in the center, the hospital behind it, and hostels in the forefront.

tools for the workers, opening boxes of medicine at the hospital, or experimenting with ten different mixes of concrete by putting them in four–inch cubes to see which was the strongest.

Otho's 25th birthday came and went on June 5 just like any other day. With Earl and the Elfgaards gone, and the Friedericks away to visit Richie and Anne at boarding school, no one in Tansen realized it was his birthday. Otho wrote in his diary that night, *"No one here knew it was my birthday, and I haven't received any birthday letters yet."* Two days later he received five cards from family and friends at home. Better late than never!

On June 20 Otho received an answer from Bob Miller at MCC regarding his request to stay longer in Tansen. Bob explained that since the Pax Program was an alternative to the draft in which the young men were required to serve, MCC's policy was that they should return home for a year after their two–year term. If after a year they still wanted to re-join Pax, they could. With the change in Otho's assignment mid–way through his term, they had already extended it one year and didn't think they should violate their policy to extend it further.

And so it had been decided. Otho would leave Tansen the following February. He wrote a letter to Paul Ruth, head of Menno Travel Services, asking him to start making travel arrangements. Realizing he had a golden opportunity to travel, Otho planned to go through Europe and Africa on his way home. In a letter home he wrote, *"In some ways I wish I could stay here and see the work completed. But I guess I'll come home and give some other fellow the chance to come out here to serve a couple years. It sure has been worth more to me than what I would ever had been able to make during these past years at home. I'll never be able to thank the Lord and you all enough for making it possible."*

Dharma Rhatna, head carpenter

Otho was disappointed he wouldn't be staying longer, but trusted God's leading through MCC's answer to his request. The work in Tansen could go on without him when it was time for him to leave. He knew God would have work for him elsewhere. Meanwhile, he would continue to enjoy his work and life in Nepal.

Kanooge, head mason

162

CHAPTER 24

Challenges Keep Life Interesting

Butwal and Tansen, Nepal; June–August 1958

Late in June, Otho prepared to go to Kathmandu to meet with all the other Pax men serving in Nepal. Mr. Benedict, who was living in Calcutta and served as director of MCC's work in India and Nepal, was planning to be there with them.

Otho looked forward to connecting with the Pax men and MCC workers. He turned over the finances to Odd to take care of in his absence, packed his bedroll and clothing for the coolie Jhaman Singh to carry the sixteen miles to Butwal, and put the rest of his belongings in boxes to protect them from the dampness during the rainy season.

Awaking early on Thursday morning, June 26, Otho ate breakfast and was on the trail to Butwal a little after six o'clock. He arrived there by a quarter after one, right on schedule. From that point on, his trip wouldn't go as planned.

On the bus ride to the airport at Bhairawa, the driver stopped six times to add water to the radiator and once to fix the steering. Once there, Otho enjoyed a cup of tea and found a place to stay for the night—a small travel trailer. He was in bed by ten, but Bhairawa was not the tranquil town of Tansen. It wasn't until after eleven that it was quiet enough for Otho to drift off to sleep.

He was up early the next morning packing his things. He stopped at a stand for tea on his way to the airport. Once there he discovered that to fly to Kathmandu he needed his passport, which he had sent to Kathmandu to renew his Indian visa. They told him to go to the governor to request permission to fly without it, but the governor wasn't able to grant it. Otho's only hope was to write a letter to Robert Fleming in Kathmandu and ask him to send his passport to him in Bhairawa.

After mailing the letter, Otho went back to the trailer to wait. He was glad he had brought along magazines to read—the *Youth Christian Companion*, *Farm Journal*, *Christian Living*, and *Gospel Herald*. The next several days would consist of sitting in the trailer reading with excursions out to eat and to buy tea at the tea stand. Each day when the daily plane from Kathmandu landed at the airfield, Otho would be there to find out if his passport had arrived.

Otho spends four nights in this trailer waiting for his passport to come by plane from Kathmandu.

Each day, Otho meets the plane from Kathmandu at the Bhairawa airfield.

By Sunday night Otho was losing hope of getting to Kathmandu. He jotted in his diary: *"Tomorrow is the last day there will be plane service in Nepal by this company. The Nepali Government wants to start it up themselves, but so far no one knows when they will start, so if I can't go tomorrow, I will have to go back to Tansen without seeing Kathmandu and the other MCC workers."*

Monday morning he was again up early, packing his things. He again stopped at the stand for tea before going to the airfield. He sat there with twenty–five others also waiting for the plane to come, but it never came. At four o'clock that afternoon, the air office men refunded their tickets. There wasn't anything left for Otho to do but go back to Tansen. He was disappointed.

He caught the first motor vehicle traveling from Bhairawa to Butwal, an old car which stopped twice on the way because of a wire shorting and lack of gas. In the same car was a young couple with a baby. They got out at the first village, but he remained in the vehicle until it arrived in Butwal at six thirty. He enjoyed a Nepali meal for supper at the Army Rest House and stayed there for the night.

Otho awoke the next morning to rain, so he waited until nine thirty to get on the trail to Tansen. He had to hike over the mountain because the river was too high to cross at Dobon. He had only crossed it once before and wasn't sure he could find his way, so he walked with nine coolies.

Their traveling style was slow. They walked for thirty minutes, then rested for twenty. During one rest period they spotted a bee's nest in a tree. Two of them took the notion to knock it down, and bees swarmed all around them. Otho and one of the coolies walked slowly away up the mountain and didn't get stung. Otho was using an umbrella, and the bees swarmed up under the top of the umbrella instead of at him. Looking back, he saw the other eight coolies running in different directions, swatting at the bees and trying to fight them off. He decided he could find his own way over the mountain and walked on alone.

It was a beautiful day. He could see the plains and Tansen from the top of the mountain Masham. As Otho walked up the hill towards home, the full moon came up and shone through the clouds. It was an uplifting end to a disappointing trip.

Carl Friedericks made a trip to Landour, India, in July. As was always the case when someone went to India, he brought back supplies and mail. One item was a suitcase full of goodies Otho's family had sent almost nine months before with three Pax men traveling to Nepal. They had left it in Delhi where Carl picked it up. Otho enjoyed going through the items in the suitcase. He noted in his diary each item: one fruit cake, one white cake mix, one can of ham, one can of peanuts, one box of sugar, one can of pork shoulder, one can of coconut, one box of cookies, one box of crackers, one box of Lipton's chicken noodle soup, one can of popcorn, three boxes of candy, tooth powder, one box of Carnations chocolate flavored milk, four books (*The New Bible Commentary* from his brother Luke, two devotional books by E. Stanley Jones from his sister Ethel, and *Walkin' Preacher of the Ozarks* by Guy Howard, also from Ethel), and six pictures from Ethel.

He would enjoy the treats from home for weeks to come. Some time later, he wrote in his diary: *"This evening Munna and I went into the Hospital to a Singspiration. After coming home I opened my suitcase and opened the package of Sunshine assorted cookies. There were 12 different kinds, and I didn't stop until I had eaten one of each. Boy they sure were good!"*

Hoping to raise chickens at Bhusaldanda, Carl had also brought back 29 hens from Landour, an incubator, and 125 eggs to hatch. Otho and Odd planned a chicken house for them. Odd drew up the plans, and Otho got several workers to build it. Meanwhile, they kept the chickens in the kitchen of the Friedericks' new house, which was still being built.

Otho and Carl set up the incubator in the shop and eagerly waited for the day when the eggs would hatch. As the three-week incubation period passed, they checked the incubator every day. But instead of chicks pecking the shells open, they started breaking and filling the air with the terrible odor of rotten eggs.

The chickens in their own new house at Bhusaldanda

For a couple weeks the shop reeked, as did Otho's room just on the other side of the partition. He was sick and tired of the awful smell. Since Carl was the one who had bought the eggs, Otho put several in a coffee tin and gave it to Ieuan Timothy to put in Carl's bedroom. That got the point across. Almost a month after they set up the incubator, they acknowledged their hatching experiment had failed. It was time to throw away the eighty remaining eggs.

Because of Otho's farm experience, he knew how to determine if an egg was rotten without cracking it open. He started examining each egg before tossing it over the hill. After not finding one that was still good, he picked up the tray and tossed the rest all at once. Exploding in mid-air, the eggs dispersed their horrible odor. The women workers covered their faces with their saris, and the carpenters grabbed an old rag and burned it to get rid of the terrible smell. By then Otho was so used to the odor, he thought the burning rag smelled much worse. He was glad to put the failed hatching experiment behind him.

Progress on the buildings moved steadily along. For weeks they worked on the plumbing. On August 21 Otho's diary entry declared a victory: *"The first house in Tansen to have running water!"* Although Otho never complained about not having indoor plumbing, he wrote that night, *"It was good to hear water running through pipes in a house again."* It wasn't a total victory, though. When they filled the pipes with water to check for leaks, there were quite a few. Otho showed one of the workers, Dil Bahadur, how to stop them, and he got busy fixing pipes.

Bhusaldanda was becoming an exciting reality, not just drawings on a page. One evening the new Governor came out to look around. It was the first time Otho had met him and found him to be friendly.

Otho kept busy that fall as the only Pax man in Tansen. He oversaw and paid the workers, fixed tools and equipment, made things in the shop, and helped with the building.

The work also had its challenges, such as the saw frame he tried to make level. It was made of four pieces of channel iron bolted together. One piece was bent one way, and another the other way, making it difficult to fit together. After hours of persistence, he succeeded in leveling it. Other challenges were a little more humorous, like the time he lost his keys. For an hour he and several of

A Nepali boy was hired to do odds and ends on the building site, including keeping the tools organized on the tool panel Otho made for the new shop.

the workers looked for them, to no avail. Just as he was about ready to head out to the trail to see if he'd dropped them there the day before, he found them — safe all that time in his own hip pocket.

Other days it seemed he got nothing done except talking over the work with Odd. The hard–working farm boy chafed at the time these discussions took, but he also realized the wisdom of planning well so the work could go on smoothly and efficiently.

He also had challenges with the workers. In September he had to dismiss some of them for the first time because of the quality of their work. One of them asked to stay for less money, but Otho declined, knowing the work was progressing too slowly as it was. A few days later he talked to all the workers about improving their work.

But there were also victories. The Friederickses moved into their new house at the end of September, signifying another part of the work completed.

Not only was progress being made for the physical well–being of the Nepali people, but spiritual progress was taking place, too. In August one of the Nepali women, Oma Shanti, was in charge of the Nepali service. She was the second convert in Tansen and had been a Christian for a little over a year, but had not yet been baptized because of the government's restrictions.

CHAPTER 25

More Changes

Tansen, Nepal; September– December 1958

Another goodbye came that fall. The Timothy family left
the early part of September, bringing more changes to life
in Tansen and to Otho's responsibilities. Ieuan had been holding Bible
study with Sil Bahadur, but after Ieuan left, Sil met most mornings
with Otho. He wasn't a Christian but wanted to learn English and
study the Bible at the same time. Otho's hope and prayer was that as
Sil studied the Bible, he would learn to know its Author and want to
follow Him, too.

In November another Pax man, Ken Stichter, would join the team
in Tansen. In preparation Otho designed and built a "double–decker
bed" for his room to give the new missionary team member a place to
sleep. He described it in his diary: *"It will be a board bed with about a
2" thick cotton mattress on it. So it will be a little hard."*

Mr. Benedict, director of MCC work in India and Nepal, was again
planning to be in Kathmandu to meet with the Pax men serving in
these two countries. Plans were again for Otho to go, and for Ken to
travel back with him to Tansen.

Otho (far left) spends time with other Pax personnel in Kathmandu: Mr. Benedict, James Miller, Ken Stichter, Willis Rudy, and Jim Witmer.

This time Otho made the trip to Kathmandu without incident. To avoid missing the flight to Kathmandu again, Carl and Betty thought he should leave on Thursday rather than Friday to make sure he caught the plane in Bhairawa since it didn't fly on Saturday and Sunday. By leaving Thursday afternoon, he made it to Bhairawa by ten the next morning and was on the plane to Kathmandu at twelve thirty.

Tom Mendes met him at the Kathmandu airport and took him to the Snow View Hotel where Otho ate a Chinese meal. The driver of Shanta Bhawan, the hospital in Kathmandu, picked him up at five o'clock to meet Dr. and Dr. Miller, Dr. Dick, and Dr. Pedley. Afterward he met Pax fellows Jim Witmer, Ken Stichter, Willis Rudy, and James Miller and spent the evening socializing with them.

Otho thoroughly enjoyed the next ten days in Kathmandu as he connected with the other MCC workers. The visit was a mixture of work and play. Otho worked on several of the mission vehicles, did wiring in one building, worked on water pipes in the hospital building, and fixed an ironing board. He also went with Mr. Bergsucker, one of the missionaries, to see a new hospital they were building. One day he hiked up the mountain behind the tuberculosis sanatorium. They had several church services and meetings. Otho showed his photographic slides at two of them and sang with Dr. Fleming and the other four Pax men at another.

It was a busy but fun time, and all too soon it was time to leave. The other three Pax men,

Otho and Ken wait at the Kathmandu airfield for their plane.

Jim, Willis, and James, took Ken and Otho to the Kathmandu airfield on Tuesday morning. It was a clear day and Otho took photos from the plane, including one of the Pokhara Hospital.

On the flight from Pokhara to Bhairawa, Otho and Ken rode in the cockpit with the pilot. They enjoyed the view from that vantage point and spotted Tansen as they flew over the town. It would take

The two Pax men spot Tansen (upper left) from the cockpit of the plane flying from Pokhara to Bhairawa.

173

another day of walking from Butwal to arrive there. Upon landing at Bhairawa, the Pax men got on the bus to Butwal and met up with Odd, who was traveling back from India. After spending the night in Butwal, the three men were on the trail early the following morning, arriving in Tansen by late afternoon.

That evening Otho read letters that had arrived while he was away: one from his mother, one from his

The bus has a flat tire on the way to Butwal.

Aunt Mary, and two from his sister Ethel. He learned that his Uncle Mike, his father's older brother, had died of a heart attack on November 1. It was now November 19, eighteen days later, and this belated news served as another reminder to Otho of the many miles that separated him from his family in Maryland.

Otho was glad to have another Pax fellow to relate to again. He and Ken got along well as they lived and worked together. In the evenings they often enjoyed playing tennis and Scrabble.

The building work continued at Bhusaldanda. They hired more workers, bringing the total to sixty–three. Otho noted in his diary, *"To keep them busy, I won't get much of anything else done from now on."* Overseeing the workers and managing the finances was an adjustment for a farm boy accustomed to doing the work himself. But the workers seemed to appreciate him, and Otho enjoyed working with them.

He and Ken spent one forenoon talking with Mr. Lutz, Betty Fredericks' father who was in Tansen on a visit, about agricultural improvements in the hills of Nepal. Otho was intrigued. Even though MCC required him to return home for a year, he hadn't given up the idea of coming back to Nepal sometime later. He confided in his diary that evening, *"To make plans to start some kind of work within the next 5 years, in some ways I would like to come back and do something like that. But I would need training in truck farming, plant husbandry, and animal husbandry."* He didn't know yet what work God had for him in the future, but it was fun to dream.

Before they knew it the Christmas season was upon them. They enjoyed caroling, giving gifts, eating together, playing games, and visiting together. Otho bought oranges and gave one to each of the workers. During their staff Christmas party, they listened to a tape from the Elfgaards, which made their Swedish friends seem a little closer. The Friedericks children gave a little Christmas program with Richard as Joseph, Anne as Mary, and Chucky and Jim as Shepherds. They asked Attan, Munna, and Otho to be the wisemen.

On Christmas morning Munna woke Ken and Otho bearing cups of coffee. While Munna was still in their room, Carl, Betty, Richie,

Otho (front left) poses with the Nepali workers after taking over some of Ragnar's responsibilities, including overseeing the workers.

Carl, Betty Anne, Jimmy (left) and the rest of the missionaries enjoy the delicious Indian meal Munna serves them at his house.

and Anne also came with coffee for them. So Otho had two cups of coffee in bed that Christmas morning. The day after Christmas, they were treated to a delicious Indian Christmas dinner at Munna's.

On December 27 Otho was beginning to be aware of the rapid passing of days and weeks. Realizing his time in Tansen was growing shorter, he wrote in his diary, *"Two days after Christmas gone by already. 7 more weeks and I'll be leaving Tansen."*

Not knowing if he would ever return and see the finished hospital building and his Nepali friends, he still looked forward to 1959, knowing wherever God led him, He had work for him to do.

CHAPTER 26

Only 45 More Days

Tansen, Nepal; January–February 1959

*B*efore Otho knew it, it seemed, the new year made its appearance. *"Yes, here it is. 1959 already. Time sure is going fast. Only 45 more days and I'll be leaving Tansen,"* he wrote in his diary.

Otho spent much of January and February wrapping up his work and handing it over to others. Some of his responsibilities were given to several Nepalis. The number of workers had risen to eighty–one, so overseeing them took even more time.

He also took time to restore his relationship with Odd Hoftun. Because of the differences in their backgrounds and experiences, Odd and Otho approached the building of the hospital complex differently — an aspect that was both an asset to the work and a challenge to the two as they worked together. As an engineer, Odd knew the wisdom of planning buildings on paper and developing strategies for running the project more efficiently. As a farmer, Otho was accustomed to jumping in and getting a job done, improvising as he went along — a method that had served him well in farming and in his earlier work in Tansen, but not as well for a building project. Odd and Otho had much respect for each other even though they had differing modes of operating. For the most part, they kept their disagreements in check, but Otho knew peace was lacking in their relationship.

The discord escalated to the point that when it came Otho's turn to lead the church service, he asked Betty Anne to lead instead because of the resentment he was feeling toward Odd. God was faithful and knew just what Otho needed. He recorded in his diary that night, *"I thank God for the sermon Betty gave and the hymns we sang all seemed to be meant for me. God sure spoke to me. Now I feel renewed again."*

That wasn't the cure–all for Otho and Odd, though. Almost a month later, Otho wrote in his diary that he and Odd *"had words, which we never had before."* Otho approached Odd to see if they could iron out their differences. Odd explained how much better it was for him to first draw out plans on paper and discover what would work and what wouldn't. He told Otho, "It's much easier to tear up a piece of paper than it is to tear down a building and start over." His explanation helped Otho understand what Odd was doing while sitting behind his desk. And Odd came to understand from Otho the importance of getting out on the project and working alongside the workers so he would know firsthand how things were going.

After each expressed themselves, Otho and Odd felt they understood each other. They prayed together and shook hands, their friendship not only still intact, but stronger than before. That discussion turned out to be invaluable to them and to the work. After that Otho often went to Odd to find out more details when he ran into difficulty explaining building concepts to the workers. He also learned from this experience the value of talking over differences with others rather than allowing feelings to fester.

During January excitement built as they anticipated the King of Nepal coming to Bhusaldanda on January 20. After a meeting to make

The missionaries and workers prepare Bushaldanda for the King's visit.

plans, they fixed up chairs for the King and Queen to sit on, a canopy for over them, and a gate for them to walk through.

On the morning of January 20, everyone was busy making everything just so. At four o'clock the King came riding on a horse. But he took the upper trail into town, bypassing all their special preparations for him. What a disappointment!

The King made speeches in Tansen and visited the girls' school. From there he and his entourage went down to Tundikhel (the open parade ground) and camped in forty or fifty tents. It looked like a small town that night with all their lights.

The next day the King and his party moved on, and Otho worked on chicken feeders. It was back to life as normal.

But three days later, thinking he might stop on his way back through Tansen, they again prepared for the King's visit. But he only came partway and then turned back. When Otho learned he was visiting the high school, he went and took pictures. He also took many photos of Bhusaldanda that day, keenly aware he would soon be leaving.

The beginning of February found Otho taking one last camping trip while in Nepal. He, Ken, Carl, Richie, and Chucky walked an hour and a half west of Tansen on the Palpa road where they made their camp. Otho slept in a hammock while the others slept in the tent.

Up at eight thirty the next morning, they were gathering sticks for a fire to cook their breakfast when they discovered they had set up camp in a Muslim cemetery. It was the only graveyard Otho saw while in Nepal since the Hindus cremate their

The gate is ready for the King and Queen.

dead. Otho soon started the campfire, mixed up the pancake batter, and began frying pancakes. They ate them as fast as he could make them. He recorded in his diary, *"We started eating at 9:30 and continued until 11:30."* They sat and talked until early afternoon, then made their way back down the trail to Tansen.

Otho was well aware his days in Nepal were fast coming to an end and had mixed feelings. After almost three years with no contact with his family and friends from Maryland except by mail, he was eager to see them again. He especially looked forward to stepping into the side door to the kitchen of the red brick farmhouse he called home and wrapping his mother in a big bear hug.

At the same time, he was reluctant to leave this place halfway around the world which he also called home. Thankfully, the choice between the two wasn't his to make and had already been made. It was his job to keep moving forward, knowing God still had work for him to do as he journeyed back to Maryland.

CHAPTER 27

So Long, Tansen!

Tansen, Nepal; February 1959

The countdown continued to Otho's departure from his beloved town in Nepal. During his last few weeks in Tansen, his friends and fellow missionaries gave many indications of how much they appreciated him and would miss him.

One day the missionaries hosted a party for the Nepali workers. Otho, Ken, and Odd wore their Nepali clothes, and Carl, Betty, Richie, Anne, Tullis, and Ingeborg wore Magar (an indigenous ethnic group) clothes. When the workers started walking up to Otho and hanging flower garlands around his neck, he was surprised to realize the party was actually for him! Each worker gave him either a flower or a garland. By the end of the day, he had over twenty–five flower garlands hanging around his neck.

Amid all the parties and busyness of finishing up his work, Otho packed, wrote letters, took lots of pictures, and had many long chats with his Nepali and missionary friends.

One evening at the Friederickses', they popped the last of the popcorn that had come in his suitcase from home. Another evening, Ram

Prashad and Kedar came out and played tennis and Ram gave him a brass wine jug. For dinner another evening, Dharma Ratna and Kanooge prepared a Nepali meal at the Friederickses' house and each gave him a brass candlestick with their names engraved on them in English. He would always treasure these items that would remind him of this place, these friends, and this period of his life that held such rich experiences and memories.

Otho packed his belongings in his blue metal trunk, making a list of all the items, and then painted his name and address on it in white. When ful-

The Nepali workers honor Otho with many flower garlands at his farewell party.

ly packed, it weighed between 140 and 150 pounds. Yogan gave him a bamboo Nepali umbrella, so he had to repack a few things to fit it in, too.

He sold his bedroll to Odd and went into town for a tetanus shot and a hair cut—all activities indicating departure was near. Needing a filling in one of his teeth, Otho visited a dentist in Tansen. He watched while the dentist melted down an Indian coin and used the silver to fill his tooth. That filling would serve him well for close to fifty years.

Just a couple days before he left, Otho took his first—and last—shower in Tansen in the Hoftun's new bathroom. The water was heated on the roof by the sun.

On Valentine's Day the entire mission staff had a party at Carl and Betty's house. They insisted Otho ride a horse from there to Odd and Tullis' house where they had a farewell party for him. It was a night full of games and laughter. Some time earlier, Otho had told them which of the chickens were laying eggs and which ones weren't. They were amazed he knew. That night, wanting to pull a joke on him, they handed him what they thought was a young rooster and asked him if it was laying. Otho told them it was, and they were astonished. Instead of picking out a rooster, they had given him a hen! The joke turned out to be on them.

They had fixed up a throne for Otho to sit in. He was to be a king and unveil various items covered with blankets that had significance

The missionaries at Otho's farewell party dressed in Nepali and Magar garb: Ken, Ingeborg, Carl, Betty Anne, Tullis, Odd, Otho, and the Friedericks children in front — Richard, Chucky, Anne, and Jimmy.

Ken and Otho say goodbye to Dharma Ratna, Kanooge, and Munna before heading down the trail to Kathmandu.

during his time with them: the little chair he had built for Lillan, the artificial leg he had made, and the incubator with a bell in it. Then Odd gave a speech and presented Otho with a brass plate.

On his last Sunday in Tansen, the sermon was about Daniel and Isaiah seeing the Lord and being called by Him. It was a fitting topic for the occasion, reminding Otho of God's calling him to Germany and Nepal and now back to Maryland. In the afternoon service, Otho sang "No, Never Alone" in Nepali and English. Yogan came to say goodbye that evening. And so ended his last full day in Tansen. He wrote in his diary that night, *"I'm wondering if this will be the last night I'll sleep in a board bed with a 1½" cotton mattress. My last night in Tansen."*

He awoke to departure day: Monday, February 16, 1959. He and Ken were planning to hike the full 150 miles to Kathmandu, giving them opportunity to visit the missionaries in Amppipal.

After breakfast and last-minute packing, it was time to leave. As Otho and Ken were ready to head down the trail, one of the workers, Bhim Bahadur Kani, put a flower garland around Otho's neck. Then, just as he had walked with others partway up the trail as they left Tansen for home, the Hoftuns, Friederickses, Munna, Dharma Ratna, and Kanooge walked along with him to the top of the hill above Bhusaldanda. There, Otho stopped and turned around. He could see all of Bhusaldanda. He raised his camera and took one last picture.

It was time to say goodbye to his dear Tansen family. Letters would keep them in contact, but this period of time when Otho had lived and worked with them in the foothills of the Himalayas had come to an end. After hugs and goodbyes, his friends turned back to Tansen where they would continue the work Otho had helped them to begin.

Munna walked a little farther with them. Then Otho realized his umbrella was broken, so Munna hurried back to get him another. He continued traveling with them until they started down the hill at Bunganese. Then he, too, said goodbye and turned back to Tansen.

Finally, it was just Ken accompanying Otho on the trail, each step taking them farther and farther from Tansen where Otho had left a piece of his heart.

Otho takes one last photo of Bushuldanda — a bare hillside when he had arrived, now dotted with buildings and the promise of much more to come for the people of Tansen.

CHAPTER 28

Just 150 Miles By Foot to Kathmandu

Trail from Tansen to Kathmandu, Nepal; February 1959

Otho and Ken continued up the trail to Kathmandu. They stopped in Ramdi for lunch and then walked on to Pullabuti. There they stayed at the same house Otho and Earl had spent the night the year before on their trip to Gorkha.

After breakfast the following morning, they started out again. Ken's stomach felt queasy most of the day and he needed to lie down several times, slowing their progress. They were halfway through the Andikola Valley when they stopped for the night.

Ken felt better the next day. They met their coolie, Porna Bahadur, at the top of the mountain. He had left the day before, carrying some of their luggage. When they caught up with him they discovered he was sick, too, and walking slowly. Otho gave him some aspirin, and then he and Ken took turns carrying Porna's heavy pack while he carried one of their lighter ones. Porna felt better after they stopped for tea, so they walked on ahead, arriving at the Pokhara hospital that evening.

Otho carries the heavier load for the coolie who wasn't feeling well.

The following morning they went over to the airfield to meet Porna and to book their baggage to leave on the next day's plane to Kathmandu. They left at noon to walk across the valley before stopping for supper and the night.

Their fifth day started out well, crossing the rest of the valley before climbing the mountain to Darabli. Ken felt fine until after they ate lunch. From that point on, they moved slowly. Ken was weak as they climbed the hill to Kuncha. They took a break for tea before starting down the hill, resting several times before stopping early. Ken opted to not eat supper, but Otho enjoyed a hot meal of rice and dal.

They were up early Saturday, getting to the Cheppi River late morning where they bathed in the river. Partway up the hill to Amppipal, Ken asked a coolie to carry his pack while he rested. Otho and the coolie continued on to Amppipal. Ken arrived a half–hour later in time for tea.

Otho and Ken enjoyed two days with the missionaries in Amppipal, attending their church services, seeing the dispensary and the school in operation, playing games, and talking.

Tuesday came, and they were back on the trail early. They descended from 4,000 feet altitude to 1,500 and then walked in valleys all day,
crossing just one small mountain. A hotel in Arughat was their destination that night. The days of continual walking were beginning to
take their toll. Ken's knee hurt, and Otho's neck and shoulders ached.

They hiked three hours the following morning before taking a
break for breakfast. Because Ken wasn't feeling well, they had to stop
for two hours that afternoon to allow him to rest before continuing on
to Tarpu. They walked through the village looking for a place to stay
overnight and get tea. No one wanted to take them in, giving them
no choice but to walk on to the next village, even though they knew it
would be dark before they got there. They weren't far out of the village
when a man came running and calling out to them. Knowing the dan-
gers on the trail at night and concerned for their safety, he told them
they should come back and stay at his house. They were most grateful.
Their host made tea for them to take on their journey the following
day, and they stretched out their beds on his porch.

Thursday morning was an early start for the two men, and they
descended the mountain in good time despite Ken not feeling well.

*Ken and Otho pause to take pictures while walking through this Nepali
village on their way to Kathmandu.*

After a delicious meal in a Nepali home, Otho settles down for the night.

After breakfast at the foot of the mountain, Ken felt worse, making their progress slow the rest of the day. They only crossed one small mountain. After passing through a nice bazaar at Trisuli, they stopped in Battar bazaar overnight, staying in the upstairs of a house where USOM (United States Operations Mission) was located.

Ken eagerly opened the canteen full of buffalo milk they had bought that afternoon, anticipating how good it would taste after a long day of hiking. He was surprised to find two chunks of butter floating in the milk. The cream had been churned into butter as they walked the rough trail that day!

Before going to sleep, Otho wrote in his diary that he had seen three things that day he had never seen before: mills run by water, a sugar cane press, and several potters making pots.

Another early start on Friday, February 27, the last day of their journey, got them to the foot of the big mountain at eight thirty and to the summit at twelve thirty, ascending from 2,000 feet in altitude up to about 7,000. They took the coolie road down to the valley and arrived at the Kathmandu bazaar. There they got a taxi to take them to Surendra Bhawan (one of the hospital buildings where the Pax men stayed)—a ten–minute drive rather than one–and–a–half hours of walking. Thankfully, Ken had felt fine the whole day.

At Surendra Bhawa Otho was surprised to see Dean Wyse, with whom he had attended EMC three years earlier. Even though Dean had been in Nepal since the summer of 1958, Otho hadn't seen him yet. The two fellows were happy to meet again and catch up.

Otho noted in his diary entry that night after arriving in Kathmandu eleven days after leaving Tansen, *"My feet are hurting a little. Outside of that I feel fine."* Not bad for having walked 150 miles of mountainous trails from Tansen to Kathmandu!

Otho points across the valley toward Pokhara.

CHAPTER 29

The Trip of a Lifetime

Kathmandu, Nepal and Calcutta, India; March 1959

When Otho knew his time would not be extended in Nepal, he worked on arrangements with Menno Travel Services for his trip home. He wanted to visit missionary friends in Kathmandu, India, several African countries, and several countries across Europe before heading home to Maryland. Realizing he might never have the opportunity again, he knew it could be the trip of a lifetime.

Otho spent a week in Kathmandu, enjoying time with missionary friends there, helping with the work, and sitting in on some meetings. While he was there, Carl and Betty flew into Kathmandu to attend a UMN meeting. Otho went with them and Mr. Bergsacker to Bhadgaon where they were building a new hospital. On the way out, Mr. Bergsacker asked Otho if he'd like to drive, but Otho declined. It had been so long since he'd driven a vehicle, and the streets of Kathmandu were full of people and animals. On the way back, though, Mr. Bergsacker slid into the back seat and told Otho he had to drive. It was the first time he had driven a vehicle since leaving Germany, and he had to drive on the left side of the road. But he did fine, and they arrived safely in Kathmandu.

Otho took his last photos of Nepal as they flew out of Kathmandu.

Three days later, on March 6, Dean Wyse and Willis Rudy drove Otho to the airport to begin the rest of his journey home. As the plane carried him out of Kathmandu and the country he had come to love, Otho pulled out his camera. He wanted to record his last views of the city and the Nepali landscape as he flew over them one last time. He hoped he would be back someday, but he didn't know if that would ever be possible.

Otho landed in Patna, India, an hour later. He headed straight to the train station where his train left at twenty after five in the evening. Twelve hours later, the train pulled into Calcutta. A short taxi ride took him to 130 Dharamtolla Street, the home of Mr. and Mrs. Benedict. Mrs. Benedict welcomed Otho warmly, *"like a mother,"* he noted in his diary.

Otho enjoyed his stay in Calcutta. He visited with the missionaries, bought supplies to ship back to Tansen, went to hear several Christian speakers, wrote letters home, made travel arrangements, shopped for things he would need on his trip home, and did a little sightseeing.

One day while he was there, he and one of the missionaries, Bill, got on a very full bus. Bill was able to get inside, but Otho stood on the steps and hung on. Another man got on the step below him. As the bus started to move, Otho felt a pull on his belt. He looked around in time to see the man jumping off the step and his own passport holder flying in the air. Thankfully, it was still attached to his belt by the chain he had used to secure it. He had been carrying it in his back pants pocket. After that he carried it in his front pants pocket instead.

Later that day a man came up to him on the street and told him, "You shouldn't carry your pen in your shirt pocket."

"Why not?" Otho asked.

"Because someone may ask to see it and then keep it," he replied. "May I see it?"

Otho pulled his pen out of his pocket and handed it to him. The man took the pen and immediately walked away, leaving Otho surprised and a bit more street wise. He never saw the man or his pen again.

After a week in Calcutta, Otho left in an air–conditioned train headed for Delhi on Friday, March 13. He made a small detour so he could visit the Agra Fort and the Taj Mahal, one of the seven wonders of the world. He wrote in his diary that night, *"The Taj Mahal sure is worth seeing."* But at the same time, the extreme poverty just outside

In Calcutta, India, Otho happens to cross paths with Fritz Mishler. a fellow Pax man he had learned to know while in Germany.

the walls of the beautiful building made of all marble dismayed him. It also saddened him to learn that the King, who commissioned the building of the Taj in honor of his wife, ordered the architect's eyes put out so he could never build another like it.

Otho spent a couple days in Delhi sightseeing and doing paperwork to obtain visas to enter the African countries he planned to visit.

On Monday, March 16, Otho was on another train, this time to Bombay. Once there he stayed at the Salvation Army house for several days getting his plane ticket from Nairobi to Rome, his ship ticket from Bombay to Mombasa, and a yellow fever vaccination.

Otho boarded the ship headed for Africa on Thursday, March 19. That evening he recorded, *"Three years ago today was the last time I saw any of my folks. Six years ago, 1953, I started farming."* Two years before on March 19, Otho had also noted in his diary the significance of that date: *"Today is quite an unusual day for me. On Friday, March 19, 1953, Lula had her sale, and I started farming. A year ago on Monday, March 19, 1956, I was with Father, Mother, Elmer, Daniel, and Amos going from Akron to Hoboken after the big snow storm and the roads were really icy."* It was the day he boarded the ship to go to Germany. Now, three years later, he was boarding a ship again on his way home. The next day, their first full day at sea, he wrote, *"Three years ago this morning at 4:00 our ship sailed from New York."* On that morning three years earlier, he'd had no idea the many experiences he'd have before seeing his family again.

He shared a berth with three young Indian men. Most of the nights they didn't come back to their room until late. The following mornings they would brag about how much they drank and how much they won or lost in the games they had played. One day one of them was telling Otho how much money he had lost the night before. He invited Otho to go with him the next night.

"No, I'm not interested," Otho told him.

He said, "You don't smoke, you don't drink, you don't gamble — you don't have any fun!"

Otho arrives in Mobasa, Kenya, after ten days at sea.

"Oh, I'm having lots of fun!" Otho replied. "I still have all my money and can freely enjoy my trip." His point was made, and the young man didn't try to persuade him again.

His spent the ten–day journey somewhat leisurely. The Indian Ocean was calm and looked almost like a sheet of glass most days. He read, updated some of his personal records, watched a table tennis tournament, and played games with other passengers. One game took place on the deck and involved throwing six–inch rings made of rope into a circle. When Otho took his turn, the ring flew overboard!

He discovered the ship didn't do laundry for its passengers so he washed his clothing by hand. Betty Anne Friedericks had encouraged him to pack lightly for his extended trip home. She had also advised him to include a Dacron shirt he could wash by hand and which would dry quickly and without wrinkles. It was invaluable advice, Otho found, as he traveled from place to place on his way home.

On Sunday he attended the church service on board the ship. Only eleven were there. An Anglican missionary serving in Bihar, India, on his way home to England, led the service. He read his sermon and prayers from a book, and the Captain played the piano.

They arrived in Mombasa, Kenya, early on the morning of Saturday, March 28. Otho was low on cash since he hadn't been able to get money exchanged on the ship due to the Easter holiday. When he de-boarded, several porters approached him offering to carry his luggage and help him through customs. Otho declined, wanting to keep what little cash he had left for other fees he might need to pay before he could get to a bank. When he got to the train station that evening, he had just enough cash to pay for his train ticket and was glad he hadn't hired the porters earlier.

He boarded a train to take him the 330 miles to Nairobi, Kenya. His trip of a lifetime was well underway.

CHAPTER 30

African Adventures

Kenya, Tanzania, Ethiopia, and Sudan; April 1959

The next morning, Easter Sunday, Otho woke on the train refreshed. He enjoyed watching the landscape slide by outside his window and seeing the many different wild animals as they traveled through the National Park.

Arriving in Nairobi at eight o'clock that morning, he got a taxi to the Africa Inland Mission Guest House. From there he planned to go to Tanzania to visit Ivan Sell, a friend from Maryland. But when Otho walked into the Guest House, he did a double take. There was Ivan, who didn't know he was coming and was equally surprised to see Otho. After catching up a little, they went to the Easter Service at the Nairobi Chapel.

This was his fifth Easter in a row away from his home community: in 1955 he was visiting relatives in Arkansas, in 1956 he was in Germany, in 1957 and 1958 he was in Nepal, and now in 1959 he was in Kenya.

On Monday Ivan and Otho went on a picnic about sixty miles west of Nairobi with some local Christian young people. There were seven carloads and two on a motorcycle — around thirty-five or forty in all.

Otho thoroughly enjoyed the day. He described his observations of Kenya in his diary: *"I got to meet quite a lot of people. From what I've seen so far Kenya is more like Europe than India. There are a lot of Indians here. They are some of the biggest shop keepers. Swahili is the main language in East Africa."*

The next day Otho and Ivan went to town to run errands. Otho made preliminary arrangements for the rest of his travels, and Ivan picked up a new International five–ton truck at the International Harvester Company and took it to a lumber company to load five tons of lumber. He had been planning to drive to Tanzania the following day, and now that Otho was there, would have a friend to ride with him. Otho noted all the new 1959 Chevrolet cars in town. He hadn't seen many late–model cars in the last several years.

The two friends left Nairobi Wednesday morning, April 1. They drove all day to Tororo, Uganda, arriving there at midnight and sleeping in the truck.

After breakfast and tea with friends of Ivan, they picked up sixty-nine sheets of asbestos roofing before leaving Tororo. They stopped at George Lanzies' at the Pentecostal Mission for supper and the night. The Lanzies were a young couple, both teachers, who had recently arrived from Canada.

On Friday Otho and Ivan went through a police check and then crossed a river on a ferry, arriving at Bukiroba, the mission near

A group of young people, including Otho and his friend Ivan, enjoy a picnic west of Nairobi.

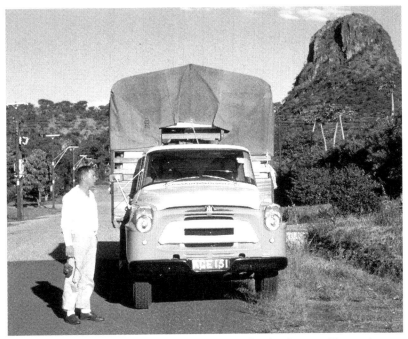

Ivan Sell stands beside the five-ton truck he and Otho drove to Tanzania.

Musoma, Tanzania, where Ivan lived. After unloading the asbestos and eating lunch, they took the truck into Musoma. Otho drove a Chevy pickup so Ivan would have a way back. The pickup's steering wheel was on the right side of the vehicle, and he wrote in his diary that evening, "The first I ever drove a right hand steering."

Otho enjoyed meeting the missionaries stationed at Bukiroba, a mission under Eastern Mennonite Board of Missions and Charities. They included Don and Anna Ruth Jacobs, George Somkers, Simeon Hurst and his wife, Alan Byler and his wife, Miss Wedger, and Mahlon Hess. He met more missionaries the following day: Levi Hurst, Miriam Buckwalter, Ruth Miller, Clara Landis, and Dr. Harold Houseman.

At the Sunday morning service, Otho gave a short talk about Nepal with Simeon Hurst translating for the Tanzanians.

He spoke about Nepal again that evening in Shirati. Otho, Dr. Houseman, Ruth Miller, and Miriam Buckwalter traveled in the mission's Volkswagen, picking up Alice Reber on the way. Once there,

John and Bertha Graybill, Nevin Kraybill, Ruth Miller, Miriam Buckwalter, and Harold Houseman set up camp on the hunting trip to the Mara jungle.

Otho met Miriam Houseman, Nevin Kraybill, and Curvin Buchen. After his talk they asked Otho questions about Nepal and the work there. He enjoyed answering their questions as he relived his time in Tansen.

On Tuesday, April 7, Otho joined a group of missionaries for a three–day hunting trip in the Mara jungle. The four men slept in a "tree house"—a three–ton truck bed in a tree — and the others slept in a Chevrolet panel truck and a Volkswagen bus.

On the first day of the hunting trip, Curvin shot a zebra. They ate some of the meat for supper and hung the carcass from a branch of the tree that held the tree house. During the night, violent shaking woke Otho and the other three men. They peered over the edge to see three lions attempting to reach the zebra. High above them, Otho took pictures. He and the others didn't get much sleep that night. When they got up the next morning, the male lion was still waiting and watching them. Curvin fired a shot to scare him, and the lion ran away.

Later they drove through the jungle, and Otho took pictures of the many wild animals they saw. They watched a dozen hippos gathered at the hippo pool while they ate lunch. Curvin shot a topi, and they ate some of the meat for supper.

That evening it rained, so they sat in the bus and sang and had a prayer meeting. When they got back to the tree house, the lions were feasting on the zebra carcass. The young men waited until they left and then hurried up the ladder to their tree house. Four more lions visited their camp that night and tried to drag what remained of the zebra away, shaking the tree and again waking the occupants in the tree house. It was the second night of little sleep.

The third day was the most profitable hunting day. Nevin shot a topi, a zebra, and a hartebeest, and Harold got two topis, a hartebeest, and an impala. After supper they processed the meat to take with them. Otho jotted in his diary before bed, *"Sure was a wonderful trip. I hope I'll have some good pictures."*

He left Shirati early the following morning, Saturday, April 11, arriving back in Bukiroba, Tanzania, before noon. He had a busy day with Ivan Sell, not getting to bed until after midnight.

On Sunday morning Otho's alarm didn't go off until almost six o'clock. He and Ivan jumped out of their beds. They had made arrangements with an Indian merchant for Otho to ride on the back of

Curvin Buchen and Nevin Kraybill with the zebra Curvin shot

his truck to Nairobi, Kenya. It was supposed to have picked him up thirty minutes earlier. Grateful it hadn't yet arrived, Otho downed a quick bowl of cornflakes and was soon out along the road with his luggage waiting for the truck. But no truck came. Eventually Ivan took him into Musoma to the truck owner's shop, and they finally left at nine thirty, four hours late. Otho sat on the back of the truck along with ten other men. They rode four-hundred miles, sitting and sleeping all day and all night on boxes of soap. They arrived in Nairobi at the Africa Inland Mission Guest House at five o'clock Monday morning, stiff and sore. When Otho tried to pay for the ride, he was surprised when they wouldn't accept any payment.

He went to town with Helge Petersen and bought three wood carvings—a lion and two deer. After supper he sang Nepali songs in his room at the Guest House.

Leaving by plane the next morning for Addis Ababa, Ethiopia, Otho gazed at the miles of barren desert land they flew over.

Clayton Keener met him at the airport in Ethiopia. Within fifteen minutes he was through customs, and they were on their way to the Mission at the Blind School for Boys. There Otho met Clayton's wife, Esther Becker, and Velma Eby. After breakfast Wednesday morning, Clayton drove Otho to the railway station where he bought a ticket for Dire Dawa, Ethiopia.

Clayton had a typewriter to send to someone at Nazareth, Ethiopia, so he sent it along with Otho. Chester Wenger and Nathan Hege met him at the Nazareth train station to pick it up. In turn, they gave Otho a pack of mail to take along to Dire Dawa. Sending items with those traveling was the easiest and cheapest way to transfer items from one mission post to another.

The train was one coach with a diesel engine on each end and held around thirty passengers. It arrived in Dire Dawa that evening. Henry Gamber was at the station to meet Otho.

As they were walking to the car, Otho looked up and saw Nevin Horst, his friend whom he was there to visit, walking toward them. He and Nevin had grown up together in the same church back in Maryland. They were both glad to see someone they knew from home. Later as they were sitting in the back of the Mission talking, they heard a noise that sounded like babies crying. "What's that?" Otho asked Nevin.

"It's hyenas out at the landfill," Nevin told him. "Do you want to see them?" They hopped in Nevin's Land Rover

Nevin Horst and an Ethiopian young man enjoy a picnic with Otho and other missionaries at Bedeno, Ethiopia.

and drove to the landfill where they saw a dozen or so hyenas picking through the garbage and eating what they could find. Back at the Mission, he and Nevin talked into the wee hours of the morning.

The next morning they drove six hours in the Land Rover to Bedeno where Nevin was serving in mission work. Otho drove while Nevin sat on the fender with a gun, watching for animals to hunt for food, but unfortunately saw none.

They spent several days at the Bedeno mission doing odd jobs and spending time with the missionaries there. He met Nevin's wife, Blanche, and their twins, as well as Mary Ellen Groth and Lois Marks.

Otho got sick Friday night with diarrhea and vomiting. Nevin gave him some pills, but Otho spent most of Saturday in bed. By Sunday he was feeling much better and spoke at the evening church service with an interpreter.

Early Monday morning, April 20, Otho and Nevin mounted mules and traveled twenty miles to the Deder Mission Station. It took all day,

Otho rides with Dr. Burkholder in the mission's Jeep up a steep road to pick up a patient.

which Otho described in his diary: *"Bedeno is about 7,000 feet. We went down to a valley to 4,200, then up over another hill to about 6,000, then down to 4,200 again. There we ate our lunch at 12:15, then went up through the valley. About 5:00 we started up the mountain. It was dark by the time we got to the top. Nevin asked a fellow if we could stay in his house for the night, but he didn't want to, so he showed us the main road. At 5 min. to 8 we saw the Deder Mission Station light. We were up to 8,000 ft. then. We arrived here in Deder at 10:00. Deder is 7,400 ft. Nevin had an altimeter along."* They stayed with Robert Garber and his wife that night.

Otho met the other missionaries at the Deder mission on Tuesday: Dr. Joseph and Helen Burkholder, nurses Lois Landis and Martha Hartzler, and teacher Mildred Histand.

After lunch he went with Dr. Burkholder to pick up a patient. They traveled twenty miles up a steep and stony hill, impassable by car. Otho was amazed how well the Jeep they were driving handled the rough terrain.

On Wednesday Nevin and his horse boy left early for Bedeno on the mules. Otho departed a short time later in a truck headed for Dire Dawa and arrived there at one o'clock. He was exhausted. After a shower he slept until late afternoon. He gave a short talk that evening at church and one of the Ethiopians preached.

Otho left Dire Dawa on Friday morning, April 24, by train and arrived in Nazareth, Ethiopia, late that afternoon. Larry Strickler met him at the station. After getting their shoes shined, they traveled by motorcycle to the mission where he met the Heges, Yoders, and Wengers.

He spent three days with the missionaries in Ethiopia and spoke about Nepal through an interpreter at an evening church service. When he had some free time, he wrote out what he wanted to tell others about Nepal since he was being asked frequently on this trip to give talks about his work in Tansen.

One day one of the missionaries did his laundry for him. Her maid started ironing his pants, but the missionary told her, "Let him iron his own pants."

There's always a first for everything, and this was Otho's first experience using an iron. He hadn't seen the need to press his pants, but cooperated with her instructions and dutifully ironed them.

On Monday, April 27, Otho flew from Addis Ababa, Ethiopia, to Khartoum, Sudan. It was the roughest plane ride Otho had experienced as they flew through a thunderstorm. The lightning flashed all around him and when it split the clouds, Otho could see all the way to the ground. At one point the plane dropped a little, right inside the streak of lightning. Otho was in awe of his Creator as he watched a thunderstorm so close.

He was grateful to land on solid ground and went to the Sudan Interior Mission. It was extremely hot there. He had toured a sugar cane factory while in Ethiopia that had felt really warm to him. He now realized it was cool compared to Sudan. Sweat poured off of him at nine o'clock in the evening while he was simply sitting in the living room. He slept on the porch where it was a little cooler.

The sugar cane factory in Ethiopia that Otho toured

Tuesday was equally hot with the thermometer registering 112° Fahrenheit. Otho shared with the Sudan missionaries about the work in Nepal and then enjoyed a tour of Khartoum, noting the contrast between the rich and poor of Sudan.

His time in Africa was coming to a close. He was scheduled that night to fly to Rome — the next destination of this trip of a lifetime. He was thoroughly enjoying it.

CHAPTER 31

Europe—Discovering Roots, Enjoying Friends

Italy, Switzerland, and Sweden; April–May 1959

Otho boarded his plane for Rome at one thirty in the morning on Wednesday, April 29. The stewardess greeted him with a request. "Follow me," she motioned to him.

He followed her to First Class where there were two young boys. She explained that the airline wanted Otho to sit with the minors since they were flying without an adult. They didn't speak English, so there was nothing for him to do but be with them. He had no idea why he was chosen or who the boys were, but was glad to help.

Once settled in his seat, Otho pulled out a book to pass the time. But it would not be a calm and relaxing flight for reading. It wasn't long until they flew into a huge sandstorm. After several hours the sand caused one of the plane's engines to cut out, forcing them to land in Wadi Halfa, Sudan, near the Egyptian border. It was four o'clock in the morning. Because the airline had to wait for tools and parts to be flown in to repair the engine, they transported the passengers to

The airline provides Otho an overnight stay on the Nile in this houseboat.

the Hotel Nile on the bank of the Nile River. Once they left the plane, Otho didn't see the boys again but knew they were being taken care of by the airline.

He was assigned a room on a houseboat floating on the Nile and slept until midmorning. Once up, he and several of other passengers from his flight traveled up the river in sailboats. They enjoyed the beautiful African scenery along the way and toured an old Egyptian temple built by Queen Hatshepsut in 1500 B.C.

After supper they returned to the airport. Their plane was fixed, and they were soon in the skies, winging their way to Rome. It impressed Otho how calmly the airline had handled the whole ordeal and paid for all the passengers' extra expenses.

They arrived in Rome a little after midnight. Otho checked into the Hotel Nord and crawled into bed at three o'clock.

He was up three hours later so he could take two bus tours of the city that day. One stop was at St. Peter's Basilica in the Vatican. When Otho got close enough to see the bronze statue of Peter, he noticed the big toe. Half had been replaced after being worn away by people kissing it, and now the replaced part was partly worn down. When he observed people walking up to the statue and bending down to kiss the toe, it reminded him of the Hindus and Buddhists in Nepal and India bowing down to worship their idols. It disturbed him so much to see Christians bowing down to an image that he turned and walked out of the cathedral to the bus and waited there until the rest were ready to leave.

He slipped into his bed early that night, tired after several nights of little sleep and full days of traveling and touring.

Rising early Friday morning, Otho made his way to the railway station and left Rome by train, arriving in Milano, Italy, mid afternoon. A Swiss boy he had met on the train in Rome helped him make the right connections. Fifteen minutes later, he was on the train for Spiez, Switzerland, and arrived there that evening.

He quickly found the train to Interlaken, Switzerland. Boarding it, he stowed his baggage and was ready to go. When he stepped off the train for a moment to read a time table, it pulled out without him, taking his luggage with it.

A typical Swiss farm with the barn attached to the house

Otho walked into the station to inform them of his dilemma. They phoned ahead to the station master at Interlaken, requesting they take his baggage off the train. He was on the next train to Interlaken an hour later and reunited there with his belongings. He settled into his room at the Hotel Jura, grateful everything had worked out that day, even if not by plan.

After breakfast Saturday morning, Otho boarded the train for Kleine Scheidegg, a mountain pass in the Swiss Alps. They climbed from the 1,850 feet altitude at Interlaken to the 6,762 feet at the top of the pass. Otho was disappointed when they got to the summit that clouds hid the terrain lying far below them. It would have been a beautiful view!

Back down in Interlaken, he meandered from the station to his hotel, stopping at several shops along the way to make purchases, including a nice Swiss watch for $18.37. He also picked out a cute little Swiss chalet music box and paid $2.28 for it. It would be a favorite of his future wife and would grace the top of their dresser for most of their married life.

For dinner that evening he savored a delicious Swiss meal at the hotel. After three years away from his Swiss–German mother's cooking, it tasted especially good to him. The dinner included potatoes with milk and peas with milk just like his mother had always prepared them in Maryland. It was memorable enough he wrote in his diary that night, *"Boy, is the Swiss food ever good. Now I know why so many of our Mennonite women are such good cooks."* He ate another wonderful large Swiss meal the following day before leaving Interlaken in the early afternoon by train.

Otho arrived in Basel, Switzerland, which bordered France and Germany, later that afternoon. At the Information Office, he asked for directions to the Mennonite Central Committee (MCC) office. He took the train to the end of the line and walked the rest of the way, stopping a couple times to ask for directions before locating it.

At the MCC office he met Mr. and Mrs. Kenneth Hiebert, Homer Amdies, Bob and Kathleen Jantzen from Berlin, and Joe Smith who was on his way home from visiting his daughter in Nigeria.

Otho visits the Elfgaard family at their home in Sweden where they reminisce about their time together in Nepal and pose for photos in their Nepali outfits.

He spent the next couple days visiting with the missionaries in Basel. One evening he showed them his slides and told them about the work in Tansen.

Just after midnight on Wednesday, May 6, Otho boarded a train to Sweden to visit the Elfgaards. He didn't sleep much during the night because the train's heater wasn't working and he couldn't get warm. They fixed it towards morning, much to his relief. The train traveled on through the day across Germany, arriving in Copenhagen, Denmark, that evening. Boarding another train, he arrived in the Elfgaards' town, Göteborg, Sweden, at a quarter to three Thursday morning.

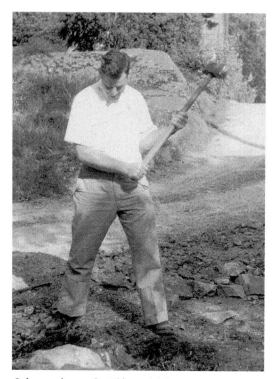

Otho works on the Elfgaards' driveway.

Otho tried to sleep the rest of the night in the Göteborg station, but it was too cold. At five thirty, he had one of the station men call the Elfgaards. Carna arrived a half hour later in a taxi to take him to their home. There they visited and caught up over coffee and bread. He would spend the next ten days in Göteborg visiting Ragnar and Carna Elfgaard and their children Lillan and Lasse. He was pleased little Lasse still remembered him and came to him right away.

The visit was filled with late nights and early mornings of reminiscing and looking at pictures of their time in Tansen. He also met many of the Elfgaards' friends and family. One day Ragnar's friend gave Ragnar and Otho a tour of the Volvo car factory where he worked. Otho found it fascinating to see how the cars and trucks were assembled.

The following day the Elfgaard family and Otho left for Stjärnorp, Sweden, for several days of sharing at a church and school about the work in Nepal. They also visited Ragnar's brother. On their way home they stopped at several of the Elfgaards' friends' homes for coffee.

The day after they got back to Ragnar and Carna's home in Göteborg, Otho worked on their driveway, breaking up the big rocks and leveling it off to make it easier for Ragnar to park there. It was the hardest work he had done for awhile, but the physical labor felt good to him.

214

While Otho was at the Elfgaards', he received a letter from Lula. It had been almost seven years since her husband Raymond had passed away. Lula had news for him and a request. She was planning on marrying a man named I. Mark Ross on June 6 and wanted Otho to be an usher. He recorded the news in his diary and wrote, *"I sure wish them God's blessing."*

Otho spent his last several days in Sweden running errands, speaking at another church, and, of course, more conversation and coffee with the Elfgaards. The ten days with this family that felt like his own passed all too quickly.

On Saturday, May 16, Otho was up early, packing his belongings back into his suitcase. After breakfast with the Elfgaards, they took him to the docks where he would board his ship for home. Within a short time he was through customs and on the ship—the *MS Kungsholm*, Swedish American Line. The Elfgaards and their friends came on board with him.

Then it was time to say goodbye to his dear friends. They left the ship to watch its departure from the docks. As the ship moved away from land, Otho stood on the deck and spotted the Elfgaards waving to him. He waved back until they were out of sight. It would be the last

The Elfgaards and their friends board the ship with Otho before saying goodbye.

he'd see this family he'd grown to love, but they would stay in contact over the years to come.

As the ship moves away from the docks, Otho sees Ragnar (upper left) waving his handkerchief and waves back until he can no longer see him or the rest of the Elfgaard family.

CHAPTER 32

Crossing the Ocean

Atlantic Ocean, aboard the MS Kungsholm; May 1959

As the last sight of the Elfgaards disappeared from view, Otho went below deck to get settled in his cabin. There he discovered one of his cabin mates was Edwin Carlson who had been in Sudan for three years with the American Mission and was now on his way home. A Swede was also in his cabin. Otho wrote in his diary that night that *"[The Swede] can't speak English so we will try to teach him some."*

The following day was Sunday, May 17, and they docked at Bremerhaven to pick up more passengers. Otho went up on deck and was surprised to see the *Seven Seas* next to them — the ship that had transported him from New York to Rotterdam in March 1956.

That evening after a welcome-on-board turkey dinner, Otho went back to his cabin. He read from his Bible and, feeling nostalgic, sang several Nepali songs.

They turned their clocks back one hour that night. The ship was taking him ever closer to home.

Experiencing seasickness the next day, Otho took anti-nausea medication that warded it off for the rest of the trip, though it made him feel tired. Not having much else to do but sleep and read, the side effect didn't matter much.

Otho took advantage of his free time to sort through his photographic slides, marking the last two boxes he'd had developed. He also pulled out 120 that Mary Cundy and Ragnar wanted copies of and got them ready to send off when he got home.

As he was walking to his room one day, he heard someone asking if he was a Mennonite. He turned to see a young man and found

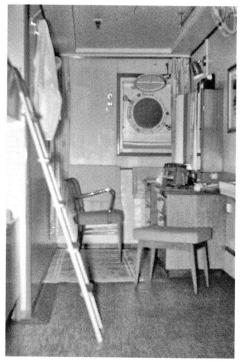

Otho's cabin on the ship where he spent time sorting through his slides

out he was Charles Miller from Meadville, Pennsylvania. He had been in Pax and had gone home in August 1956, but had traveled back to Sweden to visit his girlfriend. Now he was on his way home again to find a job. The two young men talked for a while about their experiences in Pax.

On Saturday evening the ship had a farewell dinner. The waiters came in, each carrying a plate of ice cream on a block of ice in the form of a letter. When they stood together, their letters spelled *Kungsholm*, the name of their ship.

He toured the engine room on Sunday, amazed to see the big diesel engines. Otho was particularly interested in the workshop, fully equipped with a large metal lathe and other tools to repair an engine if something went wrong.

The last full day on the ship was Monday, May 25. It was also the last day he made an entry in the diaries he'd kept for three years,

Each day on the ship takes Otho ever closer to New York Harbor and his family.

chronicling his time overseas in Pax service: *"The nicest day we had so far. I packed my suitcase and sent it up on deck this afternoon. Slept a while so I won't be so tired tomorrow. After supper I went up on deck and took a picture of the sun just as it was about ½ way down. Talked with Ed about Mission work & Mission this eve. Gave the dinner room table Steward Kr. 25.– ($4.85) tip and the cabin Steward Kr. 18.– ($3.48)."*

On Tuesday, May 26, 1959, the *MS Kungsholm* arrived in New York Harbor, and Otho walked onto US soil. A large group of his family was waiting to meet him. It was the first he'd seen any of them in over three years. He had been looking forward to this moment for a long time!

After greeting his family, Otho collected his luggage. They piled into cars and headed for Maryland. They gave Otho what they thought was the seat of honor in his brother-in-law Reuben's car: the passenger seat. But he had rarely ridden in a car during his time overseas and wasn't used to the highway speeds they were traveling. He kept pressing his feet against the floorboard of the car, afraid Reuben would run into the car in front of them. They stopped in Pennsylvania so Otho could see his Aunt Mary, his mother's only sister. When they got back in the car, he volunteered to sit in the backseat where he could better relax and enjoy the trip.

Another chapter of Otho's life was now completed and the next already begun. Once again, little did he know the joys, challenges, and experiences ahead. But he did know, without a shadow of a doubt, that the same God Who led him far away from his Maryland home was now leading him back again and still had work for him to do.

Waiting to greet Otho as he walks off the ship in New York are his parents and all but two of his eleven siblings, two brothers-in-law, several nieces and a nephew, and two of Lula's children: (front) Cheryl Kipe, Chester Horst, and Beverly Kipe; (back) Daniel Horst, Reuben Horst, Alan Kipe, Martha Horst, Elmer Horst, Mary Kipe, Anna May Horst, Karen Eby, Melvin Horst, Ethel Horst, LaVonne Eby, Pop, Mother, Lois Horst, Mark Horst, and Luke Horst.

CHAPTER 33

Back Home in Maryland

Clear Spring, Maryland; May 1959 – June 1961

Otho had missed the farm during the three years he was overseas and often looked forward to farming again. When his father asked him if he'd like to take over the home farm, he was ready and excited to do it. He kept his father's registered Guernsey cows and added the eight cows Lula had raised for him while he was in Pax.

His brother Amos, a senior in high school that year, helped to milk the cows for him. Otho would feed and bed the cattle before helping Amos finish the milking. The two brothers enjoyed working together and Otho was glad for the opportunity to build a

After Otho returned from Pax, it was just he and his youngest brother, Amos, living at home.

bond with his youngest brother who had grown up while he was away. When he had left for Germany, Amos was only fourteen years old.

One Sunday soon after Otho arrived home, he shook hands with the minister at church after the morning service. The minister asked Otho about his experiences in Germany and Nepal, and Otho enthusiastically started telling him. Then, as often happened when telling others about his Pax service, the minister seemed to lose interest.

He remarked, "I suppose you feel like they say, 'I'm glad I went, but I wouldn't do it again.'"

This astounded Otho. He looked him in the eye and said, "If I could get on the ship and go back tomorrow, I would go."

The minister stared at him, speechless, and that was the end of the conversation.

There had been a time when Otho couldn't imagine wanting to be anywhere but Clear Spring, Maryland. But now his heart pulled toward Tansen, just like it had toward Clear Spring when he lived in Tansen.

Another day soon after he arrived in Maryland, Otho met David Eby, his neighbor and former Sunday school teacher, in front of a store in Charlton. David handed him a twenty dollar bill.

Otho tried to give it back. "I don't need that, David," he protested.

With tears in his eyes, David replied, "If you don't take this, you rob me of a blessing. You gave three years serving in Germany and Nepal. I couldn't go, but you did. Please take this."

So Otho took it. It was his first lesson in graciously accepting a gift from others who wanted to express their appreciation, realizing he was blessing them by receiving it with gratitude.

That summer Dr. Carl and Betty Anne Friedericks and their children were on furlough and stayed in New York. They invited Otho to visit them for a few days before they returned to Nepal. They also asked if he'd be willing to drive them to the airport in their station wagon and then take it to Maryland and sell it. Otho gladly agreed.

It was like a little taste of Tansen to spend time with the Friedericks. Otho recounted to Carl his conversation with the preacher and

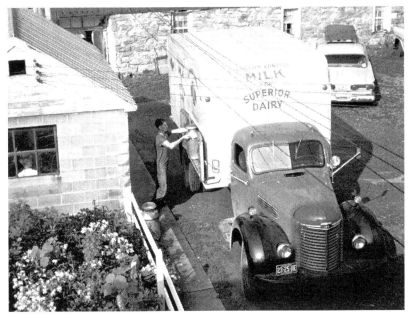

Eugene Everetts picks up milk at the Horst farm.

remarked, "It seems like the church at home changed while I was away and isn't as interested in missions as they were before."

Carl questioned him, "Did they change, or did you change?"

It was a turning point for Otho as he recognized how much he had changed during his years in Pax. Clear Spring was no longer the only place he could call home. Home was now wherever God called him.

Driving the Friederickses' car to the airport and out of New York City in all the traffic was quite an experience for someone who had just lived a couple years in a town with no vehicles. He was relieved to arrive back in Clear Spring. When he tried to sell their car in Maryland, he discovered he couldn't because of title issues. He took it to a car salesman he met at Lowville Mennonite Church in New York when he spoke there about Nepal. This man had a garage in Lowville and agreed to sell it for him. Time went by, and Otho never heard from him. He learned from someone in the Lowville church that the salesman had moved away and no one knew where he was. Otho never received payment for the car nor saw it again. He apologetically wrote to Carl Friedericks and told him the story. Carl wrote back and told him to forget about it, apologizing for Otho's trouble trying to sell it.

In the spring of 1960, Otho got ready to plant corn. He was enjoying being back in the swing of farming once again.

But one day while harrowing the middle field between the barn and the Ashton Road, the thought came to him: "What am I doing here? I'm going back and forth over this field all by myself, getting ready to raise corn to sell all for myself. The past three years I was working with people every day. Now I work only for myself and by myself. I want to be with people."

A couple weeks later, Harold Martin, the manager of Charlton Elevator, asked Otho if he would be interested in working for him part time. Otho told him what he had been thinking while harrowing the field not long before and said he would. He could have the best of both worlds by continuing the farming he loved so much while working with people at the elevator.

Not long after Otho began working there, though, he ran into a problem. Harold often needed him to work just when Otho needed to be doing something on the farm.

Also around that time, the milk inspector told Otho and his father they needed to upgrade their dairy equipment if they wanted to keep selling milk. They figured it would cost around $7,000 to meet the inspector's requirements. Pop told Otho he would upgrade the equipment if he wanted to keep milking cows.

As he thought it through, Otho realized he was enjoying working with and around people at the elevator more than farming. He and his father had a public sale that fall and sold the cattle and farm equipment. Pop rented the land to Otho's cousin Amos E. Horst to farm, and Otho started working at the elevator full time.

He recognized the encounter in the field as part of God's leading, steering him away from farming and toward the work He had for him to do next.

But first, He would lead him to find his life companion.

CHAPTER 34

Halfway Around the World and Back to Find a Wife

Clear Spring, Maryland; May 1960 – June 1961

There were several girls Otho considered dating during the early 1950s before he left for Pax. For various reasons, none of them ever worked out.

On one Sunday evening, he went to the church one of them attended determined to ask her for a date following the service. As the meeting was ending, a thunderstorm came up. Everyone made a mad dash for their cars, and there was no opportunity for Otho to talk to her.

Another time he was planning to ask a girl out after church, but her younger brother came to Otho right after the service and said, "You have a flat tire on your car." Otho went outside to look. Sure enough, his tire was flat. By the time he had changed it, his hands were dirty and everyone was leaving. He got in his car and left, too.

For those and other reasons, Otho concluded it wasn't God's time for him to marry and put dating on the back burner. During the rest of the 1950s he occasionally thought and prayed about a wife, but mostly focused on the work God had for him during that time.

Otho met several nice young women during his years in Pax but didn't feel the Lord leading him into a relationship with any of them. Several times while in Nepal, he wrote names of girls he knew on pieces of paper, put them in a cap, and pulled one out. But it didn't help him settle for any particular girl, and he again put dating on the back burner. With the full and active life he led in Tansen, it wasn't difficult for him to focus on other things.

A year after Otho came home, Raymond's youngest sister Dorothy asked if she could borrow his pictures of lepers in Nepal. She was teaching at Paradise Mennonite School and wanted to show them to her students who were knitting bandages for lepers. Otho told her he would bring them to her house so he could explain them to her.

That following Wednesday after supper, Otho cleaned up from a typical work day on the farm and put on nice clothes. He knelt beside his bed and prayed for God's guidance in whether he should ask Dorothy for a date that evening. Even though she was five years older than he, Otho had learned to appreciate her over the years and knew she had many of the same viewpoints and values he did.

Before he left his room, Otho's brother Melvin came in and asked, "Where are you going all dressed up?"

"Dorothy Eby wants some of my leprosy pictures to show her class, and I'm taking them down to her house for her," Otho told him.

"People will talk," Melvin warned.

"That's okay," Otho responded with a shrug and ran down the back stairs of the farmhouse into the kitchen where his mother was working. He told her where he was going. She didn't say a word, just gave him a big smile, and Otho knew he had her blessing.

When he arrived at Dorothy's house in Maugansville, he drove to the back and parked in front of her garage. Although she knew he was coming sometime, she didn't know when. She was upstairs sewing and heard a car in the driveway below. Looking out the window, she

Dorothy's home in Maugansville, Maryland, where she lived in one half of the house with her Uncle Henry and Aunt Minnie Hostetter in the other

saw it was Otho. When he got to her kitchen door, Dorothy was holding it open and inviting him in. She escorted him into the living room and they sat together on the sofa, looking at his pictures. They had a good time together that evening as Otho described the photos to her.

Walking through her kitchen to leave, he stopped and asked her the question heavy on his mind, "If you don't already have plans for Sunday evening, may I pick you up and take you to church?"

"Yes," she agreed with her sweet smile, and the following Sunday evening, May 15, 1960, was their first date.

After that evening, they dated regularly.

Otho realized God had been working through the years to bring them together. Since Dorothy's father, Samuel Eby, was the minister at Otho's home church, Otho had known Dorothy all his life. He remembered her as a young girl with one long braid, and Dorothy recalled being a guest in the Horst home and seeing a little red-haired boy peering over the table.

Later, when Otho worked for her brother Raymond, he interacted a lot with Dorothy and the rest of the Eby family.

After Raymond died in 1952, and after Dorothy's mother died almost a year later, Dorothy would often spend weekends with Lula and her children. The two sisters-in-law grew close during those years as they supported each other through their losses.

Since Otho lived at Lula's during that time, he learned to appreciate Dorothy's sweet and gentle spirit, her compassion for others, and her desire to serve the Lord above all else.

In January 1956, Dorothy was a student at Eastern Mennonite College in Harrisonburg, Virginia, when Otho attended a six-week Bible term there. One day after lunch, they crossed paths in the hallway and stood talking for quite a while. He discovered they shared similar viewpoints on various subjects important to him, and that she was interested in growing spiritually and helping others, just as he was. That conversation gave him an even deeper appreciation for her.

There were several humorous incidents that took place before they started dating. One happened the Sunday before Otho left for Pax. He was at Lula's house and Dorothy was there, too. Lula had taken nurses' training to become an LPN after Raymond died and was working the night shift at the hospital. She had worked Saturday night so was staying home from church to sleep. The plan was for Otho to drive her car and take the rest of the family to church. When he went out to the car, Lucille, LaVonne, and Karen were sitting in the backseat. He got in the driver's seat and Lynn, who was now five, insisted his Aunt Dorothy sit between him and Otho so he could sit by the window. Dorothy was a little self-conscious about this arrangement, wondering what people at church might think if they her saw sitting next to Otho. But she said nothing and scooted into the middle of the seat next to him.

The only correspondence Otho and Dorothy had while he was overseas was once when Lynn wrote Otho a letter and insisted that his

Aunt Dorothy also write something in the letter. So she did.

Several days after Otho returned home from Pax, he rode along with Lula and her fiancé, I. Mark Ross, to Harrisonburg, Virginia, for Lucille's graduation from Eastern Mennonite High School (EMHS). I. Mark told Otho he was glad to meet this man for whom Lula had delayed their wedding so he could attend. Otho enjoyed the time traveling together in the car to get acquainted with I. Mark and catch up with

Dorothy May Eby

Lula. When they arrived in Harrisonburg, Dorothy, who was there attending Eastern Mennonite College (EMC), joined them for supper at the EMC dining hall where the students ate family style. Lucille, serving as their hostess, seated Otho and Dorothy on one side of the table and her mother and I. Mark on the other. She took the place at the head of the table.

Dorothy wrote in her journal afterward, *"That was the first I had seen Otho since he came home May 25th. He seems the same except naturally he is more mature."*

In the year following Otho's return from Pax, a group of young people held weekly church services at the Hagerstown jail on Saturday evenings and would gather at Dorothy's house afterward. Otho was often part of this group.

Also during the summer of 1959, a car load of youth went to a Mennonite youth convention in Ohio. On the way home, Otho was driving while all the passengers were sleeping except Dorothy. They talked for quite a while, becoming increasingly familiar with each other and discovering their many similar beliefs and perspectives.

In March 1960, a group of young people planned to travel together to Virginia for Lucille's nurse capping ceremony. As the time got closer, one by one all but Otho and Dorothy canceled because of other obligations. So the two of them drove alone to Harrisonburg in her car and again enjoyed the time talking and getting better acquainted.

After they started dating in May 1960, some of their family and friends thought because they were "older" they would get married in a few months. But it didn't happen quite that fast.

Otho and Dorothy on their wedding day

On Sunday night, September 3, 1960, Otho was walking with Dorothy through her kitchen to the back door to leave when he heard himself say, "What would keep us from planning our lives together?"

Dorothy looked up at him with her sparkling deep brown eyes and replied without hesitation, "I'm all yours!" Right there in her kitchen, they sealed their commitment with their first kiss.

On June 17, 1961, they exchanged vows in Dorothy's living room in a simple wedding ceremony with both their families and a few friends present. They left afterward for a honeymoon through the New England states.

When they returned, Otho moved into Dorothy's home in Maugansville, writing in her guest book the first day, "I'm here to stay!"

He has often enjoyed telling people, "The Lord took me halfway around the world and home again to find a wife." His and Dorothy's single days were over for the next fifty years, but God still had lots of work for them to do, both individually and together.

CHAPTER 35

The Next 50 Years and Beyond

Belize, Maryland, Florida, Arkansas,
and Virginia; 1961–2018

*J*ust four months after Otho and Dorothy's wedding, Hurricane
Hattie hit the tiny country of British Honduras (now called
Belize) on October 31, 1961, devastating thousands of homes. Aware
of Otho's interest in mission work, Adam Martin, director of MCC's
work with the Colony Mennonites in British Honduras, asked Otho if
he would help rebuild homes in Belize City for two months with Mennonite Disaster Service (MDS).

Although they had only been married a few months, Otho and
Dorothy felt God was leading him to to go, so he did. Dorothy stayed
home to continue teaching at Paradise Mennonite School. During the
two months Otho was away, from mid–December 1961 to mid–February 1962, the newlyweds kept up a steady stream of written correspondence, each writing almost every day. Otho discovered if he wrote one
way on the one–page airmail forms with a blue pen and wrote over

the blue ink in the opposite direction with a red pen, he could write twice as much in his letters and Dorothy could still read every word. Despite missing Dorothy for those two months, Otho knew without a doubt God had led him to serve that time in British Honduras. That became even more clear as they recognized later how it was a stepping stone for the future work God had for them.

Dorothy, Myron, and Otho stand in front of Mennonite Center where they lived and worked in Belize.

On July 31, 1962, Dorothy gave birth to their first child, Myron Otho. As they would do with each of their children, they knelt down beside their sofa the same day they brought him home from the hospital and dedicated him to the Lord, asking His guidance and help in raising him.

When Myron was only three months old, Mennonite Central Committee asked if they would move to Belize City, the capital of British Honduras, to manage Mennonite Center. There Otho served as manager of the store on the street level of Mennonite Center, and Dorothy served as hostess of the hostel on the second floor. They lived in rooms on the second and third floors.

Mennonite Center served the Colony Mennonites who lived in their own remote farming communities in British Honduras. The store at Mennonite Center provided a venue to sell their farm products while the hostel gave them a place to stay when they came into the city. Otho and Dorothy also helped start a Bible study in a community in Belize City that later became a church.

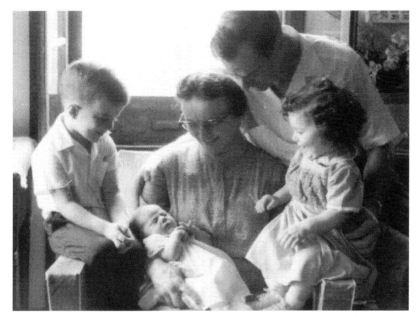

Myron, Dorothy, Otho, and Fern welcome the new baby Carna in the living room at Mennonite Center the day she came home from the hospital.

During the five years they served in Belize, two little girls were born to them: Dorothy Fern (whom they called "Fern") on August 7, 1964, and Carna Rebecca on March 22, 1966.

When Dorothy was pregnant with their fourth child, God led them back to Maryland in December 1967.

Otho and Dorothy rented a house in Maugansville, Maryland, after their return to the States. After three months they bought a house in the rural community of Mt. Lena, about twenty miles from their hometown of Clear Spring. They became active in the little church called Mt. Lena Mennonite. Their property was at the edge of Greenbrier State Park and had space to raise a few calves and grow a garden. Otho worked at Maugansville Elevator while Dorothy tended to their family at home.

Dorothy gave birth to their fourth child, a sweet little girl named Karen Marie, on March 2, 1968. They were now a happy family of six, involved in work and ministry they enjoyed and living on an ideal property to raise their family. It seemed life couldn't be any sweeter than it was right then.

But on November 3, 1968, tragedy struck. Eight-month-old Karen swallowed a brad paper fastener that lodged deep in her throat, blocking her airway and preventing removal by family members who valiantly tried to save her.

Her death was a shock to them, their families, and the community—a healthy baby girl taken in an instant. But Otho and Dorothy felt a deep peace in their grief. They had long ago entrusted themselves and each of their children to the God they had chosen to serve and knew Karen was now forever safe in the arms of Jesus.

They buried her tiny coffin in the cemetery of Mt. Zion Mennonite church with a headstone that reads, "At Home in Heaven," and ended her service with the congregation singing victoriously:

"Lift your glad voices in triumph on high
For Jesus hath risen, and man cannot die
The being He gave us, death cannot destroy
Sad were the life we must part with to-morrow
If tears were our birth-right and death were our end
But Jesus hath cheered the dark valley of sorrow
And bade us, immortal, to heaven ascend
Lift your glad voices in triumph on high
Jesus hath risen, and man shall not die."

Dorothy had learned from the loss of her parents and brother that life goes on after the passing of a loved one. She still had three children to care for and knew she couldn't become lost in her grief. Her sister Marie came and put away the baby crib that sat beside their bed and helped her fold the tiny dresses and pieces of clothing to give to others. She kept several little outfits as reminders of the precious life God had given them for a short time.

The Sunday after Karen's funeral, Otho went to the front of the church to open the morning service, but no words came. Then, as he regained his composure, he began singing, "God Moves in a Mysterious Way," and the congregation joined him.

Several days before Karen passed away, Otho's eighty–year–old Aunt Carrie had also died suddenly. Otho has often observed that

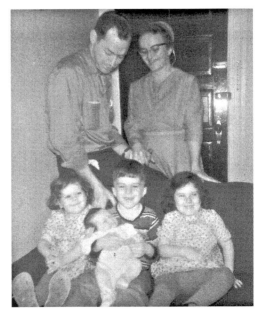

Otho and Dorothy with all four of their children: Carna, Karen, Myron, and Fern

most of us are of an age somewhere between eight months and eighty years, and each one of us could die just as quickly as little Karen and Aunt Carrie. "How important it is," Otho says in reflecting on their lives, "that we are ready when our time comes by choosing to place our faith and trust in Jesus."

At eight months Karen died a missionary, inspiring several by her short life to follow Jesus. Otho's youngest child's work on earth was finished, but God still had work for him and Dorothy to do.

More change was on the horizon. It wasn't long after Karen went to live with Jesus that Lloy Kniss, bishop of the Washington-Baltimore District, asked Otho to serve as pastor of Gaithersburg Mennonite Church in Gaithersburg, Maryland, a northwest suburb of Washington DC. It was one of nine churches in the Washington-Baltimore District under the Lancaster Mennonite Conference of churches headquartered in Lancaster, Pennsylvania.

In late August 1970, Otho and Dorothy moved with their family to Gaithersburg, still a small town on the outskirts of Washington, DC. Otho was licensed as pastor of Gaithersburg Mennonite Church on July 19, 1970, and ordained on February 17,

Otho and Dorothy with their children Carna, Myron, and Fern not long after moving to Gaithersburg, Maryland

1974. Because being pastor of the little congregation was not a paid position, Otho also worked full–time at Gaithersburg Lumber, which was later renamed "Barrons." He was grateful it was a short walking distance from both their home and the church and that his employer gave him flexibility to leave when needs arose within the congregation.

Gaithersburg was home for Otho and Dorothy for the next thirty years. As the little suburb grew into a city around them, they ministered to the ever–changing population of a transient area. Otho and Dorothy deeply loved the people they served. The doors of their home were open to anyone, including the teenage boy who ate almost every Sunday lunch at their house and the elderly lady who stayed with them after heart surgery. Sitting at the kitchen table watching Dorothy prepare a meal, she remarked, "Now I know why everything you make tastes so good. It's made with love!"

On Monday morning, March 18, 1975, Otho received an unexpected phone call at work from his brother-in-law Alan Kipe. Otho's parents and sister Ethel had been involved in an accident in Orange-burg, South Carolina, on their way home to Maryland from Florida. Pop, age seventy, had died instantly. Otho's mother was severely injured with a fractured femur and was in the hospital, and Ethel had sustained a broken wrist. The next day Otho and his brother Elmer and sister Mary were on the road to South Carolina.

His mother spent several weeks in Orangeburg hospital with her leg in traction and Ethel faithfully by her side, unable to attend her husband's funeral. When they flew home, Otho and Dorothy picked them up at the airport and took them to their house for several days. Then, when his mother felt ready to face her house in Clear Spring without her husband of almost fifty years, Otho drove them home. In spite of the doctor's warnings that she might never walk again, Otho's mother — a strong resilient woman — made a full recovery.

On the Sunday before Otho's parents had left for Florida, Otho and his family had visited his parents. After supper Otho said to Pop, "We'd better soon leave so you can go to church this evening."

"We can go to church anytime, but we can't always visit with you," Pop told him. It turned out to be Otho's last visit with his father and one he treasured. Pop told him that evening that there were times he had been concerned about the spiritual well-being of his children, but that he was so glad they were now all serving the Lord.

In 1977 Otho, Dorothy, and several others from neighboring Mennonite churches formed Gaithersburg Christian School in the Gaithersburg Mennonite Church building. Otho served as administrator and school pastor. Dorothy, a life-long advocate of good education, served as the principal and one of the teachers. All three of their children attended and graduated from the school. After twelve years, the school closed in 1989 as more families were choosing to homeschool their children. Dorothy became a homeschool coordinator, advising

The staff and students of Gaithersburg Christian School during its first year. Dorothy is first in the second row; Myron second from left in the third row; Fern third from left in the back row; Carna far right in the back row.

homeschooling families and serving as a liaison between them and the public education system. Facilitating learning, both in and out of the classroom, was one of her life's passions, with Otho's full support.

By the end of 1992, Otho and Dorothy's little nest at home was empty. They watched as each of their children drove away to new ventures, with their blessing.

Myron attended Eastern Mennonite University in Virginia and later graduated from Rosedale Bible Institute (now Rosedale Bible College) in Ohio. On a tour with the Rosedale Chorale during the summer of 1986, he met Cathy Yoder from Hutchinson, Kansas, and they married on June 6, 1987. Six children were born to them in the years from 1988 to 2000: Joel, Nathan, Kara, Daniel, Luke, and Melody. Myron worked as a trim carpenter before starting Jehovah Jireh Farm near Dickerson, Maryland, in 1997, which continues to produce organic eggs and other food products. He also enjoys writing in his spare time.

Fern lived in Ohio for thirteen years following high school, graduating from Rosedale Bible Institute and Cedarville College and working on staff at Rosedale as the librarian and writer/editor of the school's publications. She moved back to Gaithersburg in 1996 and served as the writer, editor, and webmaster for a nonprofit organization before beginning her own website design company and online ministry to singles. Fern now works as a freelance writer and life purpose coach and lives in a small apartment attached to Otho's house, doing what she can to assist him in his elder years.

Carna also graduated from Rosedale Bible Institute and then worked as a graphic artist at Gospel Echoes in Goshen, Indiana, and then at Gaithersburg Gazette after moving back to Maryland. She married Dennis Reitz, also from Gaithersburg, on June 8, 1991, and became a homeschooling mom to their children: Timothy, Ranita, Alyssa, Benjamin, and Valerie, born in the years from 1992 to 2004. They moved to Fauquier County, Virginia, in 2000. Carna currently enjoys teaching a ladies' Sunday School class in their church, Dayspring Mennonite.

Otho retired from his job at Barron's in 1993 — but not from the Lord's service. God still had work for him to do. On January 17, 1993, Otho and Dorothy handed the keys of Dogwood Cottage to Dennis, Carna, and little Timmy to live in during the next two years while they served with Rosedale Mennonite Missions.

Otho and Dorothy's first assignment was in Southmost, Florida, as leaders of a team cleaning up and helping to rebuild after Hurricane Andrew that hit Florida on August 24, 1992. In the eight months they were there, they rebuilt Southmost Mennonite Church in Florida City and helped repair several homes.

On September 21, 1993, they moved to El Dorado, Arkansas, for their second assignment, and served as house parents for a voluntary service unit of young people and as chaplains at Holden Memorial Nursing Home. It was a challenging but rewarding time as they again built friendships and ministered to the people there.

They moved back to Gaithersburg on January 10, 1995.

Otho's mother's health was declining, and he and Dorothy took turns with other family members in giving his sister Ethel reprieve in her full-time care of her mother. During that same time, Dorothy's only sister Marie was also declining in health from terminal cancer, and Dorothy spent time helping her daughters as they cared for her.

On the morning of April 1, after seeing all twelve of her children within the prior twenty-four hours, Otho's mother passed away with several of her children at her side. She was ninety-one. Around mid-morning, Dorothy got the call that Marie had taken a sudden turn for the worse. She was able to be at her sister's bedside along with Marie's husband and some of her children when Marie, too, breathed her last. It was a time of tremendous loss for Otho and Dorothy and their family.

Otho was ordained on June 2, 1996, as a bishop in the Washington–Baltimore District of Lancaster Mennonite Conference, providing oversight and support for five churches. He viewed his role as being an encourager to them. Dorothy accompanied him as he visited the churches and enjoyed interacting with the people. As they had done before in the places they served, Otho and Dorothy deeply loved and cared for the people, and were appreciated and loved in return.

In 2000 Gaithersburg Mennonite Church closed. A Hispanic congregation began to meet in its building, serving the growing Hispanic

*Otho and his siblings celebrate their mother's eighty-eighth birthday on
January 17, 1992: (back) Irvin, Elmer, Melvin, Martha, Otho, Dan, Mary,
Mark, Luke, Amos; (front) Ethel, Anna (Otho's mother), Lois.*

population that now characterized Gaithersburg. In the same year,
Otho officially retired from his role as a minister and bishop in Lancaster Mennonite Conference. God's work for Otho in Maryland was
finished, but He still had work for Otho to do.

In August 2000—almost thirty years to the day they moved to
Gaithersburg in 1970—Otho and Dorothy moved to the Shenandoah
Valley of Virginia near the little town of Broadway, just north of Harrisonburg. God blessed them with a beautiful hilltop property with such
gorgeous views of the mountain range to the east that the previous
owners had aptly named it Grandeview. They attended Morning View
Mennonite Church and appreciated and enjoyed the people there.

After a couple years in Virginia, Otho was asked to serve as interim
pastor of Salem Mennonite Church, a little church that was a forty

minute drive into the hills of West Virginia. From 2002 to 2004, Otho and Dorothy served and loved the Salem congregation and were loved in return. Otho worked with them to appoint a team of elders to provide leadership, and they again attended Morning View.

In 2003 Otho was appointed as the assistant overseer of the Mountain Valley Mennonite Churches. Again Dorothy faithfully traveled with him as he visited the various churches. Roland Good, one of the pastors at Morning View, once joked to Otho during this time, "Retirement isn't going so well for you, is it?" But he knew Otho hadn't retired to Virginia to sit on his haunches. Otho had taken God seriously in the pasture field after Raymond died in 1952 and knew that as long as he had breath, God would continue to have work for him to do. Although he hadn't expected it would be church leadership again, he was willing to do whatever God called him to do. And so when Salem again needed a pastor in 2008, Otho filled the role a second time until January 2011 when Craig Good became their permanent pastor.

Otho was now officially retired from church work a second time. He was seventy-seven and Dorothy was eighty-three. The large house

Otho and Dorothy with the Salem congregation in West Virginia

Otho and Dorothy's family celebrate their fiftieth wedding anniversary:
Cathy Horst, Myron Horst, Melody Horst, Luke Horst, Daniel Horst, Fern
Horst, Joel Horst, Kara Horst, Dorothy Horst, Nathan Horst, Otho Horst,
Ranita Reitz, Valerie Reitz, Carna Reitz, Tim Reitz, Ben Reitz, Dennis Reitz,
and Alyssa Reitz.

and property were becoming a challenge to maintain. They decided
to sell Grandeview and move east across the mountains close to Carna and her family near
Bealeton, Virginia.

But then they were dealt
a terrible blow. Dorothy
was diagnosed with stage
IV lung cancer on Sep-
tember 7, 2011. Although
it was a shock to them and
their family, they accepted
it gracefully, trusting God's
purposes and plan for
them as they had all their
lives. They could see even
more clearly why God had
already set things in mo-
tion for them to move.

On January 19, 2012,
the moving trucks drove

Otho and Dorothy on their fiftieth wedding
anniversary, June 17, 2011

243

them away from Grandeview and over the mountains to their new home. Dorothy loved their little house and named it "Cozy Cottage." Otho was relieved to have a smaller house and property to maintain. Carna's husband Dennis got to work overseeing a garage addition that would also house a workshop for Otho and a small apartment for Fern.

But before it was completed, Dorothy developed pneumonia and was hospitalized, declining rapidly. She spent those last days in the hospital as she did all the previous days of her life: pouring love on those around her and inspiring trust in Jesus by her own complete trust in Him. On the evening of March 29, 2012, with Otho and her children gathered around her hospital bed, Dorothy's sweet, gentle spirit slipped away to be forever at home with Jesus. Dorothy's work on earth was finished. It was a tremendous loss for Otho, but he also recognized that God still had work for him to do.

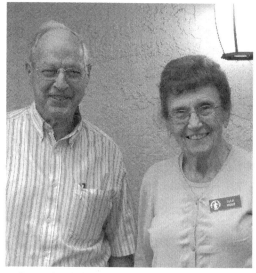

The close relationship both Otho and Dorothy had with Lula and her family continued throughout the years, with Lula living in Sarasota, Florida, for most of them. The fortitude and grace she demonstrated during Raymond's illness and passing was evident throughout her lifetime. She lost her second husband when their sons Conrad and

Otho and Lula always enjoyed visiting when they could in the years after he worked for her and lived with their family. This photo was taken in 2013 during their last visit before her passing.

Otho and Fern with Lula's six children after her memorial service: Conrad Ross, Otho Horst, Lucille Horst Schiefer, Karen Moyer, LaVonne Amstutz, Fern Horst, Lynn Eby, and Conrad Ross.

Curtis were teenagers. As before, she relied on the Lord and His care for them, and He proved faithful to them. Lula worked as a nurse until she was in her eighties and then remained active living in her villa at Sunnyside Village Retirement Community in Sarasota.

In 2013 Fern spent several months in Sarasota helping to care for a terminally ill friend and was grateful for the opportunity to better get to know her Aunt Lula who was special to both her parents. At the end of Fern's stay, Otho flew to Florida for what turned out to be his last earthly visit with Lula. He enjoyed the time with her and her three sons and their families who also live there.

At age ninety-eight, Lula went to her heavenly home with Jesus on February 15, 2017. Otho and Fern joined her family and friends for a beautiful memorial service and celebration of a life well-lived.

Otho continues to live at Cozy Cottage and attends Dayspring Mennonite Church where Dorothy's body was laid to rest with a headstone that says, "Safe in the Arms of Jesus." It comforts him to think of her being with Jesus, and that Jesus is also with him.

The farm boy in him still comes out to play as he enjoys working outside as much as possible, mowing his yard with his little John Deere tractor and maintaining his house and property with the help of family. When he gets tired, he sits in his recliner and enjoys reading biographies that tell of God working and leading in others' lives.

He continues his lifelong mission of encouraging others to live for Jesus. Whether it is his neighbors, his family, someone he meets in the store, or people at church, Otho has a smile and an encouraging word for each one. Part of the work God still has for him is praying for others. Each evening after praying for his children and grandchildren, he pulls out prayer lists from missionaries, mission agencies, and churches, as well as church and ministerial directories. These serve as prayer reminders as he prays for the people listed in each one.

Even though he isn't able to do as much physical work, Otho still firmly believes that as long as he is here, God has work for him to do. He believes the same is true for everyone. As he encourages others, he often tells them of his encounter in the pasture the morning Raymond died when God spoke those eight little words that changed his outlook and the course of his life: **"I still have work for you to do."** He usually concludes, "That has stuck with me all these years, and I believe as long as a person has life, regardless of what age they are, what condition they're living in, or how sick they are, God has a purpose and a plan for them."

The righteous thrive like a palm tree
and grow like a cedar tree in Lebanon.
Planted in the house of the Lord,
they thrive in the courts of our God.
They will still bear fruit in old age, healthy and green, to declare:
"The Lord is just; he is my rock,
and there is no unrighteousness in him."
(Psalm 92:12–15 CSB)

The Work in Nepal After Otho Returned Home

Nepal; 1950 – 2018

In the months after Otho left Tansen in February 1959, eight Nepali workers affected by the lives and faith of the missionaries they worked for, decided to follow Jesus and were baptized. This was a brave step for them to take since the Nepali constitution stated that everyone was free to practice their own religion as handed down from ancient times but not to change their religion nor cause someone else to change their religion. The new believers were born Hindu.

Not long after this, Prem Pradhan, a former Gurkha soldier in the British army who converted to Christianity in India and returned to Butwal, Nepal, as a missionary in 1959, brought his ill wife to Tansen to the hospital. While there he discovered the small group of Nepali believers. He and his wife moved to Tansen in the Spring of 1959 to be their pastor. From prior experiences in China and India, Carl Friedericks had learned it was best that foreigners not dominate the Nepali church. The missionaries were delighted that Prem agreed to be the pastor.

Prem baptized the new believers on August 21, 1959. Afterward, they and the missionaries gathered at the Elfgaards' home for communion and a meal together, all eating together without the caste restrictions of the Hindu religion from which they had converted.

The converts' neighbors and others in Tansen got wind of the conversions and reported the new Christians to the governor. Carl Friedericks received a letter from him requesting the names of all those who had become Christians that worked for the mission. That same evening, the believers gathered in the Friederickses' home for their weekly prayer meeting, and Carl told them about the letter he'd received from the governor.

"What should I do about it?" he asked the new Nepali Christians.

"Give them our names," they told him. So Carl wrote them down — some worked in the hospital, some in the building program, and some worked in the missionaries' homes.

On November 21 the new Christians were called to the police station and questioned individually why they had become Christians. Their response was that as they learned about Jesus they had found peace in their hearts. They were all put in jail without a trial. One woman was pregnant and delivered her baby in jail one month later, another had a twenty–one–day–old baby girl with her, and another woman had two young sons. Each day the prisoners were told that if they denied Jesus they could return home, but no one denied Him.

The missionaries felt terrible. They were free while the Nepalis they had introduced to Jesus were in jail for their faith. Each day they visited the prisoners to cheer them, taking along whatever they could to make their lives a little easier. The missionaries would go to the jail to encourage the imprisoned Nepali Christians but would return home encouraged by them.

The prisoners began having daily Bible studies together. During their time in jail, they studied through the New Testament three times. One who had attended Bible School in India declared that one month in jail was better than a whole year in Bible School because he was learning so much. Other prisoners joined their Bible studies and some became Christians, too.

In June 1961 Otho received a letter from Mary Cundy saying that the King had sent a four-man committee to look into the cases. The missionaries had hopes they would release the Christians, but the committee's attitude was just the reverse. They insinuated the missionaries were foreign spies, serving up sugar-coated poison in the shape of hospitals, libraries, etc. It seemed Satan had triumphed, and the missionaries felt discouraged. But as they turned to the Lord, He assured them that "the triumph of the wicked is short" (Job 20:5).

They had one glimmer of hope when thirty-one other prisoners in the Tansen jail were released in celebration of the King's birthday. Soon after this, one of them came to the missionaries asking to buy a Bible, hymn book, and a copy of Pilgrim's Progress. While in prison, he had been meeting with the Christians in prison with him and now wanted to keep on reading and studying the Bible. *"So 'the wind bloweth where it listeth',"* Mary quoted from the Bible in her letter to Otho. *"Praise Him that nothing can bind His Spirit."*

Ragnar Elfgaard worked diligently with the government to get the prisoners released. They were finally freed eleven months later except for Prem Pradhan who was serving six years for causing others to change their religion. Prem chose to look at the bright side, saying, "It's okay, because now people around the world are praying for us!"

After everyone but Prem was released, he became lonely without the others and asked God how he was to survive another five years alone. The Lord told him, "There are many people with you. Why not have a church here?"

So he told the other prisoners about Jesus and helped to care for those who were sick. As they became Christians, they encouraged each other. But the authorities were unhappy he was converting yet more people to Christianity. They put him in solitary confinement in a room where they put the bodies of prisoners who died in jail and chained his right hand to his right foot and his left hand to his left foot.

One day Prem was praying out loud in his cell. The guard came running and asked him who he was talking to.

"Jesus," was his reply.

"How did He get in here?" the guard demanded.

"He's with me all the time," he told the astonished guard, who was looking around with his flashlight to see if he could find the intruder.

"I can tell you how to find Him," Prem offered.

He had the guard's full attention. Prem explained how the God, Jesus, took on the punishment for the sins of all people when He died, and that He resurrected from the dead and now lives through His Spirit in those who believe in Him. He further explained that God will not judge the believers according to their sins, but according to Jesus' perfection.

As it had been for Prem as a Hindu first hearing about Jesus, this was incredibly good news for the guard. Rather than being caught in the despairing cycle of reincarnation based only on his own inadequate merit as the Hindu faith taught him, he could ask the perfect Jesus to be his stand-in when it came to judgment. Then, not only would he live again after death, but would live forever with God in Heaven — not as an insect or some other lowly creature facing an endless cycle of death and reincarnation as the Hindu faith taught.

It was clear to the guard. He laid down his rifle and knelt down, asking Jesus to be His Savior and come live with him, too.

In the six months Prem was held in that room alone, all four guards who watched him became Christians when Prem told them about Jesus. The government became frustrated that no matter what they did to Prem, he converted others to Christianity. So they moved him to another prison near Kathmandu. He had to walk, in chains, the 150 miles over mountainous terrain from Tansen to Kathmandu.

When Prem and his guards came through Bhusaldanda as they left Tansen, he was allowed to stop and say goodbye to his friends. The missionaries and hospital staff sang and prayed with him and gave him some gifts. Prem was grateful to be making this difficult journey since it gave him the opportunity to tell others about Jesus all the way from Tansen to Kathmandu. He said, "I look on this trip as a missionary journey and I am in good spirits."

In the new prison in Kathmandu, Prem continued to tell others about Jesus. Many more became Christians. The Nepali government moved him from prison to prison to keep him from converting prisoners to Christianity. But their plan failed. Approximately seventy–five guards and prisoners from different Nepali tribes and regions became Christians because Prem told them about Jesus. After their conversion he would have Bible studies with them, and they grew strong in their faith. As these prisoners were released, they took the good news of Jesus back to their people, and Christianity spread like wildfire as their friends, family, and neighbors saw how much they had changed after they had put their faith in Jesus.

The government came to realize that Prem was converting more to Christianity in prison than he was outside, so they released him before the end of his sentence. He would go on to tell many more about Jesus and be jailed numerous times during his lifetime. As a result, Christianity continued to spread throughout the country of Nepal. He became known as the "Apostle to Nepal" and his facinating story is told in his book (Prem Pradhan, *Apostle to Nepal,* Seedsowers 2008).

In 1990 a political revolution took place and Nepal became a secular multi–party democracy instead of a Hindu kingdom. However, laws prohibiting proselytism continue to concern Nepali Christians, with the Nepali parliament passing an even stricter law in late 2017. But even with these restrictions, Christianity continues to spread — from only one known Nepali Christian in 1950 to estimates of up to three million in 2018, and from no church in Tansen to seven today.

The work in Tansen to improve the health and lives of the Nepali people has also expanded. Letters from the Tansen missionaries to Otho after he returned to Maryland kept him updated on developments.

EIGHT LITTLE WORDS

In a letter dated June 19, 1961, Odd Hoftun wrote:

"The rains have started and we have been working hard to get roof on everything. We have now only the operating section of the main building left, but lots of inside work left in the wards, etc. The last residential building is almost completed. So Bhusaldanda has changed quite a bit since you left. The main building looks quite impressive."

Two months later Odd updated Otho again on the progress in a letter he wrote on August 12, 1961:

"The main hospital building is now under roof more or less, but quite a bit of work remains inside. About half of the building is taken into use by the hospital. We have also decided to put up another couple dera units with about 20 rooms for patients' relatives. That is the end of the hospital building program.

Then comes the school which we plan to build on the bare knoll just below Bhusaldanda. The building will continue over several years, and when the whole project is completed, it will have a total floor area twice as big as the hospital. But by then the hospital too may have grown. We plan to have about 160 students finally—in 20 classes. Otherwise the work is growing fast in whole Nepal.

The last is a scheme for aviation service between the stations and the man behind this idea is Carl, of course.

The workshop is going on about as usual. We have taken in Dil Bahadur's [one of the workers who had worked with Otho and later been imprisoned as a new Christian] *younger brother who seems to be an able fellow too. And Bir Bahadur from Kalimpong is working as a carpenter and will later on be a teacher in the school. Otherwise most of the old ones are still there.... The hospital office has been moved up into the new building, and the godown building there is now only medicine stock and office for the building department."*

Carl and Betty Anne also wrote to Otho about their two–hundred mile trip by foot into the remote Doti district of Nepal with their young family and a few others to explore the possibilities of supplying much–needed medical help to the area. No one area was populated enough for a hospital like they were building in Tansen, but Carl had a vision for smaller medical units to reach people further out. *"We are convinced we can't walk between,"* Carl wrote in his letter, *"so let us fly! We are in fact contacting the Mission Aviation Fellowship with this in mind. We know several possible landing strips."*

In another letter from the Friedericks on September 24, 1961, Betty Anne wrote that plans were proceeding for the medical expansion into Doti. The Tansen hospital would serve as the base for clinics there, which Carl would visit by air. She wrote, *"Here in Tansen the building is continuing and the doctors are busy with patients.... A great deal of work needs to be done in public health as ... so much of the illness could be prevented. Better diet would also help the people and we are glad that we are getting a start in Agriculture work in Gorkha and we hope in other places, too."*

She then wrote about her parents retiring from missions in Korea and coming to Tansen for six months to study the agricultural needs and help the Tansen missionaries start agricultural work to improve the lives and health of the Nepali people.

Another letter from the Friederickses in May 1962 informed Otho that Missionary Aviation Fellowship had come and looked at the proposed landing strip locations and agreed to join them in the work.

And so the work in Tansen continued and grew. Bhusaldanda, once a forsaken barren hill that no Nepali wanted because they considered it haunted, is now covered with buildings including the hospital compound and many houses.

Today the United Mission Hospital Tansen, as it is now named, has its motto printed in bold letters in both Nepali and English on the front of the main building: *"We serve, Jesus heals."* In Charlie Friedericks' tribute given at the memorial service of his father Carl Friedericks on August 15, 2015, he said, "The hospital itself stands as a statement to the redeeming work of Jesus, who brought Light to the darkness, and hope to an area once filled with fear."

The hospital celebrated its 60th anniversary in June 2014. From its humble beginnings as a clinic when Otho was there in the 1950s, the hospital in 2014 had twelve senior doctors, sixteen residents and interns, and one hundred sixty–five beds, as reported in the hospital's 2014 Friends of Tansen publication.

Otho is grateful to have been a part of the beginnings of this work that has brought light and life to the people of Nepal who only a short time before had been living in darkness, closed off from the rest of the world and all the benefits of modern medicine, agricultural methods, and spiritual enlightenment. Their ignorance and superstition had enslaved them to poverty, sickness, and despair.

After Otho returned home and became engaged to Dorothy, Munna wrote her a letter dated June 12, 1960, that reflected Otho's influence on him and the people in Tansen. He wrote, *"Otho is my fast–friend in Christ. I love him and I have learnt many things from him. I can never forget him and always liked to be with him and it is my great desire to see him once more. He was a really spiritual boy among all the others. And ALL in Tansen loved him. We all missed him very much after his departure."*

Otho and the diverse group of missionaries he served with in the 1950s planted many seeds that are bearing fruit today. Little did they know as they interacted with the Nepali workers who became Christians soon after he left, how the number of Christians in Nepal would grow into hundreds of thousands. And little did they know as they started the building of the hospital compound it would now serve over 100,000 inpatients and outpatients per year at the hospital itself and thousands more in the surrounding areas.

It serves as a regional hospital for an area of almost a million people and its services include surgery, pediatrics, general medicine, obstetrics, gynecology, dentistry, a burn unit, a postgraduate training program for physicians in internship and residency programs, and clinical training for nurse anesthetists and midwives. In association with the hospital, Tansen Nursing School opened in 2000 to train certificate–level nurses for western Nepal.

The hospital in 2018 now employs over four hundred Nepalis and twelve mission appointees from six different countries who serve mainly in teaching or supportive roles. Not only has the United Missions to Nepal brought much–needed western services to Nepal, it has brought education and employment by empowering the Nepalis to provide these services to their fellow citizens.

In 1997 Otho received a phone call from a friend, Carol Herr. Her husband Jim, a physician, was planning to take a year sabbatical and spend it with his family in missions overseas. His assignment was to serve as a doctor at Tansen Mission Hospital. "Do you know where Tansen is?" Carol asked Otho, knowing he had served in Nepal.

Otho could hardly believe his ears when he heard the word, "Tansen." He excitedly told her that was the hospital he had helped build almost forty years before.

In January and February 1998, Otho and Dorothy visited the Herrs in Tansen. Otho was pleased to see the completed hospital buildings and the continuation of the work he had helped start, and Dorothy was delighted to experience in person the place she had heard so much about.

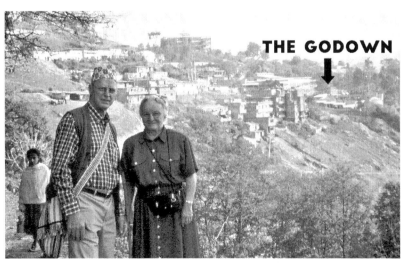

THE GODOWN

Otho and Dorothy with Bhusaldanda in the background — a bare hillside when Otho arrived there in 1956.

One evening Otho shared his photos with the UMN personnel who were interested in hearing about the start of the work in Tansen. He encouraged them in their current work with the words from 1 Corinthians 15:58: *"Be ye stedfast, unmoveable, always abounding in the work of the Lord, forasmuch as ye know that your labour is not in vain in the Lord."* He felt blessed to be able to see firsthand how his own labor there forty years before had not been in vain.

The contrasts between life in Tansen from the 1950s to the 1990s were striking to Otho. In the summer of 1958, he and the Elfgaards were the only ones living on the hillside of Bhusaldanda; in 1998 over a thousand people lived there. Forty years before he had to walk at least sixteen miles to get to Tansen; in 1998 he arrived by jeep, driving right into the streets of Tansen that had never seen a wheeled vehicle before he and Earl pushed the wheelbarrow they made through the town in 1958. On February 16, 1959, he left Tansen and walked ten days to get to Kathmandu on his way home to the States; on February 17, 1998, he and Dorothy rode the Buck (bus owned by UMN) and arrived ten hours later in Kathmandu.

One change that was especially surreal to Otho was sending emails to his family at home in Maryland. The mere moments it took to send and receive a reply was a sharp contrast to the weeks of waiting for letters to make their way to and from Maryland in the 1950s.

While it intrigued Otho how much had changed, he also noted those that hadn't—like seeing the mostly unchanged Godown wedged between more modern buildings and sighting Carl's Shopsmith in the workshop.

Otho and Dorothy also spent several days in Kathmandu. Unexpectedly, their visit coincided with Odd and Tullis Hoftun—a special treat for Otho.

Fifty years after Otho and Earl Schmidt said their goodbyes on the trail just outside of Tansen as Earl was heading home, they met again at the Mennonite Nepal Reunion at MCC headquarters in Akron, Pennsylvania, July 30 – August 3, 2009. It intrigued Dorothy to see the two men, then in their seventies, pick up their friendship right where they'd left off on that trail in Nepal over fifty years earlier. Now Earl and Otho occasionally chat by phone, talking just as freely as they did over sixty years ago when they lived and worked together in Tansen.

On October 9, 2009, Otho and Dorothy drove to a restaurant in Maryland to meet Carl and Betty Anne Friedericks, now in their nineties, who were making a cross–country trip in their motorhome from their home in Stanwood, Washington. It was the first Otho and the Friedericks had seen each other since Otho had taken them to the airport in New York the summer of 1959 on their way back to Nepal. It was also the first and only time Dorothy visited with these dear friends of Otho. They had a wonderful time together.

In 2014 Carl and Betty Anne once again made a cross–country trip and attended the Mennonite Nepal Reunion in June 2014 at MCC in

Otho enjoys a visit from Betty Anne and Carl Friedericks in June 2014.

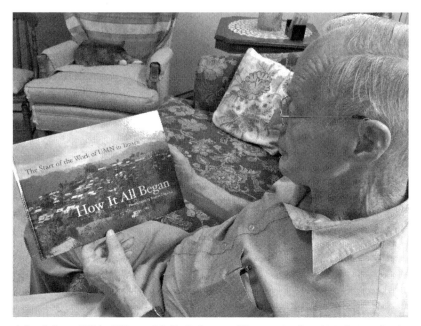

A book from Lillan Elfgaard full of photos of Tansen in the 1950s brings back many wonderful memories for Otho.

Akron, Pennsylvania, which Otho also attended. They traveled back to Virginia with Otho, stopping at his son Myron's farm in Maryland and enjoying a meal with him and his family. Then it was on to Cozy Cottage where Otho's daughters Fern and Carna and Carna's family also enjoyed a meal with them. It was a treat for Otho's family to meet this special couple they'd heard so much about all their lives.

Carl passed away a year later on July 3, 2015. His work on earth was finished, and what a legacy for the Lord he left behind. Otho talked to Carl on the phone several times in the weeks before his passing. It blessed him to hear Carl express the peace he felt as he faced the end of his earthly journey and knew what was waiting for him beyond.

Otho received a precious gift in the mail in September 2015 — a book by Lillan Elfgaard who now goes by Marie Schön, her married name. Lillan was just five or six years old when Otho left Nepal in 1959 but remembers Otho well. She wrote in an email to Otho that he and Earl were her heroes when she was a little girl in Tansen. Her book, *How it All Began*, is about the early years of the work in Tansen when Otho and the Elfgaards served there together. Reading it and seeing the many photos she included brought back many memories for Otho. Ragnar passed away in 2002, and Carna turned ninety-three on September 16, 2017. She sent Otho her warmest greetings via her daughter's email correspondence with Otho.

In February 2017 Jim Herr was back in Tansen for a visit and sent a few photos to Otho via Facebook Messenger. Moments later, due to Facebook's notification system, he realized that Otho had just opened his message and was viewing the photos. Jim picked up his cell phone and called Otho. The contrast in communication between when he lived in Tansen in the 1950s and present day could not have been more striking to Otho. Being able to send photos from Tansen in-

Jim Herr sent this photo to Otho in February 2017 — the present–day view between the Godown and the hospital.

stantaneously and then talk to the recipient moments later was mind boggling.

One of the photos Jim sent Otho was of the new tennis court built on top of a water tank which was installed in 2016 on top of the old tennis court Otho helped to build while he was there in the 1950s. Due to the huge demands for water in the hospital and the lack of it during the dry season, an engineer named Ed Kramer designed a rainwater harvesting tank to take advantage of the abundance of water during the monsoon season. The new tank has the capacity to hold 396,258 US gallons of water.

And so God's work continues in Tansen, Nepal. It also continues all around the globe through the people who served there together in 1956–1959 and who continue to serve Him until their work here on earth is finished and God calls them Home.

This photo from Jim shows the new tennis court next to the Godown with the huge rainwater harvesting tank sandwiched between it and the old court.

Otho's Reflections

Those eight little words I heard from the Lord in 1952 after Raymond died, "I still have work for you to do," have come to my mind often throughout my life, especially when making decisions.

The first decision came when Lula's brother asked me to stay and work for Lula. I knew without a doubt that was the work God had for me then. And, when she decided to have a farm sale in 1953 and asked me to farm the farm on shares, my answer was an easy "yes." I had peace knowing I was doing the work God had for me to do.

Those words also came to mind many times when I was asked to go somewhere I hadn't been before or to do something I had never done before. As I would remember those words from the Lord, "I have work for you to do," it was much easier to consent to go and to do, knowing He had work for me to do.

I believe that is true not just for me, but for everyone, and that as long as a person has life, regardless of what age they are or what condition they're living in or how sick they are, God has a purpose and a plan, something for all of us to do.

I have visited a lot of people in hospitals and nursing homes over the years, and many times they ask, "Why am I still here? Why doesn't the Lord take me Home?" My answer to them is, "God has a purpose and a plan for you to be a blessing to others, just as you are to me right now."

When I was pastor at Gaithersburg Mennonite Church in Gaithersburg, Maryland, in the early 1970s, Pastor Reid at the Derwood Baptist Church helped me discern that my spiritual gift is serving. That freed me to understand that my way of doing and saying things come from my gift of serving. I have always enjoyed doing and saying something to help and encourage others.

Soon after Otho bought his first car, a 1940 Plymouth, he purchased this small motto to hang from his rearview mirror. He has hung it in each of his vehicles since, including his current 2006 Dodge Caravan. It reminds him of God's leading in his life— past, present, and future!

When Dorothy and I came to the end of our two-year voluntary service term in Arkansas, we wondered what the Lord had next for us to do. We both felt He was telling us to be an encouragement to others in their service for the Lord.

In the summer of 2016, my daughter Fern, who is a life purpose coach, asked me some questions about my life and then came up with a life purpose statement for me: *"My life purpose is to experience joy and contentment trusting in Jesus and yielding full control to the Holy Spirit, so that with integrity I can help others and encourage them spiritually."* It has been a real blessing to me ever since. I also look back and see that has been my purpose all my life. It has freed me, knowing I can still live my purpose even now in my 80s. I've memorized it and enjoy sharing it with others as an encouragement to them to discover their life purpose.

I realize that I can't always do what I used to do and sometimes I need to say "no." Brian Good from Broadway, Virginia, helped me understand this when he told me one day, "Your biggest problem is that you can't say 'no'." Thank you, Brian, that has helped me ever since. I can't do the physical things I used to do, and God doesn't call me to do everything, but I can still encourage others and live His purpose for me.

Soon after Dorothy died, I read that joy is a choice. I decided that I would choose joy. There is real joy in following the Lord's leading, in being where He wants us to be, and in doing the work He has for each one of us to do.

I have no regrets. I thank the Lord that He has led me this far and I know He will lead me on from here. My prayer is, "Lord, I'm available to do what you want me to do."

Always remember that God always has something for each one of us to do.

Otho with his family in 2007: (back) Tim Reitz, Carna Reitz, Dennis Reitz, Valerie Reitz, Joel Horst, Myron Horst; (middle) Alyssa Reitz, Ranita Reitz, Fern Horst, Kara Horst, Daniel Horst, Nathan Horst, Cathy Horst; (front) Ben Reitz, Otho Horst, Dorothy Horst, Melody Horst, and Luke Horst

Fern's Reflections

Bealeton, Vrginia; March 2018

"Sing it again, sing it again!" I can remember it almost as though it were yesterday—the twinkling eyes and smiling face of my father as Myron, Carna, and I begged him to sing "Kushiko Dihn Ho" for us. He would start singing the Nepali words and we'd join in:

Kushiko dihn ho, kushiko dihn ho,
djabba Ishu le mero,
djaba Ishu le mero paapa dhoe.
Un le sekaio, un ko ichanosaar, un lai prartna garno,
dinau aanan ma nai basau.
Kushiko dihn ho.

I grew up hearing not only my father's favorite Nepali song over and over but also the stories from this book as he told them. I don't know which I enjoyed more: hearing them again and again or watching others listening intently as they heard them for the first time.

As my niece Alyssa and I worked on this book, reading his diaries and the letters he faithfully sent to his mother who just as faithfully kept them, each story fell into its context of the bigger story that is my father's life. In its entirety, it is a story I'd never heard before, and I feel honored to serve a part in preserving it so others can know it, too.

In many ways these stories are not just my father's. They are also mine. They formed the man who became my father and who had—still has—a tremendous impact on me. And as I reflect on the periods of his life before and after Nepal, I see how God was weaving my mother's story into his long before either of them realized it and that it is from this even bigger story that I was born and nurtured.

But my father's stories go far beyond anything to do with me. As I read with interest about the Nepali workers who were baptized within months after my father left

Otho and Fern in 1967, cropped from a family photo taken while missionaries in Belize

Tansen and noted some of their names in his diaries, I realized that his interaction with them likely had a part in their decision to follow Jesus. I found myself humming the old campfire song, "It only takes a spark, to get a fire going...." Indeed, the spark that was my father's work in Tansen combined with those of the other missionaries started a fire that has brought light and hope to the people of Nepal—spiritually, medically, economically, and other ways.

As he went back to Maryland and then to Belize and the other places God has led him, sparks from his work in those places have started other fires, and only God knows the full impact they have had—and will have for years to come.

As far as the eight little words God spoke to my father after Uncle Raymond passed away, it is easier for me to accept the hope in them than the finality of the four words preceeding them: "Raymond's work is finished." They appear contradictory to my human perspective that

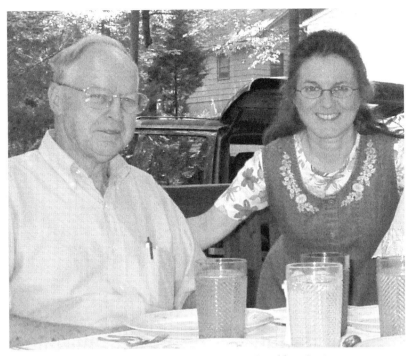

Otho and Fern in 2007 at their family cottage at Sparkling Springs near Singers Glen, Virginia, where the Horst family spent many happy vacations.

Aunt Lula and her children still needed him here. But as I look at the rest of Aunt Lula's life, I see how faithful God was to her and to her six children — each one of them gracious, compassionate, and strong individuals who are impacting the world in positive ways despite losing their fathers when they were young. It is obvious God has had work for them to do, too, and still does.

And that is true for each of us and the impact I pray this book will have on its readers — that God has a unique purpose and plan for each of our lives and meaningful work for us all to do.

Alyssa's Reflections

Remington, Vrginia; March 2018

I love a good story. There's just something about it that thrills me deep down inside.

When I was growing up, stories were common at Grandma and Grandpa's house. We would snuggle up next to Grandma and she would read us book after book. She had a way of reading stories that brought them to life! Grandpa, on the other hand, had a way of telling stories from his younger days that riveted us. I remember many times sitting around the table or the living room listening to Grandpa's stories. And somehow, even though I had heard them before, they never got old.

They still don't get old.

More than twenty years of hearing them and now several years of reading and transcribing his diaries and letters, picking his brain for details, and putting them all into book form, and I still love when Grandpa gets that little smile on his face and sparkle in his eye as he tells a story. Sometimes he points at me and says, "I think she knows my stories almost as well as I do," because of all the time I've spent on this book. The truth is, I'll never be able to tell his stories like he does. Besides, there's nothing like firsthand experience! Fern and I did our best to write this in his storytelling style, but there's just no way to

Otho and Alyssa in 1998 at Dorothy's 70th birthday party

completely recreate it. I wish every one of you could just sit down with my grandpa and hear these tales from his mouth!

As I've worked on compiling Grandpa's stories and experiences in the Pax Program, I've had the privilege of seeing some of the things that make him who he is today—and therefore have immensely affected my life. The experience in Raymond's field and those eight little words have affected how he has lived every day since then. His experiences leading devotions and giving messages to small groups of missionaries prepared him for his roles as pastor and overseer. His friendships with people from others nations and denominations gave him a love and acceptance for all people. The large variety of items he had to make in the shop in Tansen gave him the ability and creativity to fix almost anything. Whenever something broke when I was little, my mentality was, "If Mommy can't fix it, Daddy can; if Daddy can't fix it, Grandpa can; if Grandpa can't fix it, it can't be fixed!" While I realize now that Grandpa can't fix everything, I'm still amazed at all the things he can fix!

ALYSSA'S REFLECTIONS

It has been an honor to write this book! All the long hours, neck aches, and tired eyes have been worth it. But before I stretch and close my laptop on this one last time, I want to leave you with two things:

First, God has a purpose for you. He created you and puts breath in your lungs every day because there are people He wants you to touch for His glory; and second, your Heavenly Father is writing a story for you that is far more incredible and fulfilling than you could ever imagine! Don't lose heart on the hard days; He's still working. Keep pressing on!

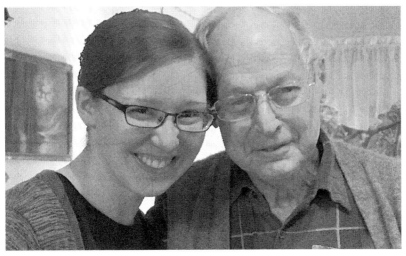

Alyssa and Otho in 2018 at Cozy Cottage, Bealeton, Virginia

Made in the USA
Middletown, DE
09 September 2018